MONETARY MANAGEMENT

Basic Concepts and Practices

Kurada T S S Satyanarayana
MBA., M.Com.
Senior Research Fellow, DCMS,
College of Arts and Commerce, Andhra University

Prof A. Narasimha Rao
M.Com., MBA., Ph.D., FCMA
Principal, College of Arts and Commerce,
Andhra University

NOTION PRESS

India. Singapore. Malaysia.

ISBN 979-8-895567-49-4 (PaperBack)

ISBN 979-8-895567-50-0 (HardCover)

Dedicated to MY PARENTS

Smt. Satya Anantha Lakshmi
&
Sri. Venkateswara Rao

Detailed Table of Contents

Contents

Preface

Monetary management is at the core of economic stability and growth, influencing every facet of a nation's financial health. As economies around the world continue to evolve and integrate, understanding the key concepts and practices of monetary management has become more essential than ever.

This book, Monetary Management: Basic Concepts and Practices, is designed to offer readers a foundational understanding of the fundamental components of monetary management. By focusing on the essential mechanisms and policies that guide monetary systems, this book provides practical insights into how central banks and governments navigate the complex world of financial regulation, economic growth, and stability.

The first chapter explores the role of the Central Bank, delving into its critical function as the authority that regulates the supply of money and oversees monetary policy implementation. The second chapter focuses on Monetary Policy, illustrating how these policies are used to control inflation, stabilize currency, and foster economic growth.

The third chapter covers Open Market Operations, explaining how these operations serve as tools for central banks to influence liquidity and interest rates in the economy. Chapter four turns its attention to Credit Policy, addressing the strategies employed by governments and financial institutions to manage credit availability, interest rates, and lending practices.

Finally, the book concludes with Fiscal Policy, a key aspect of monetary management that examines the government's use of taxation and spending to influence economic activity and achieve long-term growth objectives.

Whether you are a student, professional, or anyone with an interest in monetary management, this book offers a concise and comprehensive guide to understanding the fundamental practices that shape modern economies. My hope is that readers will find the concepts and strategies presented in this book useful and applicable to both academic study and real-world financial management.

I would like to extend my gratitude to all those who have supported me in bringing this work to life, and I hope it serves as a valuable resource for anyone eager to learn more about the dynamic field of monetary management.

Kurada T S S SATYANARAYANA

Author

Acknowledgments

The completion of this book has been an enriching experience, made possible by the invaluable support and guidance of many individuals, to whom I am deeply indebted.

First and foremost, my heartfelt gratitude goes to **Prof. A. Narasimha Rao, M.Com., M.B.A., Ph.D., FCMA,** whose mentorship, expertise, and unwavering support have been pivotal in the development of this work. As the Research Director and Principal of the College of Arts and Commerce, his insights and constructive feedback have profoundly shaped the direction of this book. Prof. Rao's passion for knowledge and dedication to nurturing young minds have been a source of immense inspiration, and I consider myself fortunate to have had the opportunity to work under his esteemed guidance.

I would also like to express my sincere appreciation to my co-research scholars, **Battula Vijay Kiran, Kumpatla Jaya Surya, Teki Yaswanth Kumar, and Arangi Venkata Ramana**. Their encouragement, collaboration, and shared dedication have played a significant role in the creation of this book, providing much-needed motivation throughout the process.

A special thank you goes to my younger brother, **Praveen Srikanth**, for his unwavering support, which has been a pillar of strength during this journey.

This book is dedicated to my parents, **Sri Kurada Venkateswara Rao** and **Smt. Bolloju Satya Anantha Lakshmi.** Their unconditional love, belief in me, and support have been the foundation of my achievements. My mother, a dedicated Teacher, has been a constant source of strength, guiding me with her tireless dedication and care. This book is a reflection of their influence, and I am forever grateful for their presence in my life.

Kurada T S S Satyanarayana

CENTRAL BANK

Learning Objectives:

- *Understand the central bank's fundamental role in a nation's monetary and financial system, focusing on its functions in regulating and supervising the economy.*
- *Learn about the structure, objectives, and key responsibilities of the Reserve Bank of India (RBI), including its traditional, developmental, and supervisory roles.*
- *Explore the various functions of the central bank, specifically the RBI, and how they differ from those of commercial banks in India.*
- *Analyse the importance of the central bank's objectives, including price stability, economic growth, and the management of monetary supply.*
- *Compare the distinct roles and functions of central banks and commercial banks, emphasizing their complementary roles in supporting the Indian financial system.*

CENTRAL BANK

The banking system of a country can work systematically in coordinated manner, only if there is an apex institution to direct the activities of the banks. Such apex institution is popularly known as 'central bank'. The central bank of the country is an autonomous institution, entrusted with powers of control and supervision. It controls the monetary and banking system of the country.

After World War II, the importance of central banking grew significantly, and several developments in international monetary policies shaped the creation and functioning of central banks worldwide.

In 1929, the International Monetary Conference held in Brussels recommended the establishment of a central bank in every country. This conference emphasized the need for a strong financial institution to regulate monetary stability and oversee banking activities within each nation.

As a result, the Reserve Bank of India (RBI), the central bank of India, was established in 1935. The RBI was tasked with managing the country's monetary system, issuing currency, and overseeing the banking sector, playing a pivotal role in India's financial and economic management.

The Bank of England, established in 1694, is often referred to as the "mother of central banks" because it pioneered many of the key functions associated with central banking, such as acting as the government's banker and managing monetary policy. It laid the foundation for modern central banking practices, which have been adopted globally.

In France, the Bank of France was founded in 1800, following the French Revolution. It played a crucial role in stabilizing the French economy by managing the nation's currency and acting as a lender to the government.

The United States established its central banking system in the form of the Federal Reserve Banks in 1914. The Federal Reserve was created to provide a more stable and secure financial system in the U.S. and to regulate the country's monetary supply and interest rates.

These developments highlight the global trend toward creating central banks to ensure financial stability and economic development, particularly in the wake of major global events like World War II.

A. Central Bank:

According to Smith, 'the primary definition of central banking is a banking system in which a single bank has either complete control or a residuary monopoly of note issue'.

H.A. Shaw defines a central bank, 'as a bank which controls credit'.

According to Samuelson, 'a central bank is a bank of bankers. Its duty is to control the monetary base and through control of high-powered money to control the community's supply of money.

Following are some of the central banks of different nations:
1.Federal Reserve Bank of USA

The Federal Reserve Bank (Fed) is the central banking system of the United States. It was created in 1913 by Congress to provide the nation with a stable and flexible monetary and financial system. The Fed is made up of twelve regional banks that are responsible for implementing the policies set forth by the Federal Reserve Board.

The Fed's policies are often closely watched and can have a significant impact on the economy. The Federal Reserve Chairman, who is appointed by the President and confirmed by the Senate, is the face of the Federal Reserve and provides testimony to Congress twice a year on the state of the economy and monetary policy.

2. European central bank

The European Central Bank (ECB) is the central bank for the European Union and is responsible for the monetary policy of the Eurozone. The bank was established in 1998 and is headquartered in Frankfurt, Germany. The main objective of the ECB is to maintain price stability within the Eurozone, which means keeping inflation low and stable. The ECB has several tools at its disposal to achieve this goal, including setting interest rates, buying and selling government bonds, and providing financial assistance to member states.

The Governing Council is the main decision-making body of the ECB, which is made up of the six members of the Executive Board and the governors of the national central banks of the Eurozone countries. The President of the ECB, who is appointed for a non-renewable term of eight years, represents the bank at the highest level and presides over the Governing Council.

The ECB also has supervisory responsibilities for the banking sector in the Eurozone, it conducts prudential oversight of banks and other financial institutions to ensure that they are operating safely and soundly and that they are following the rules and regulations.

Overall, the ECB's main goal is to maintain price stability, promote the smooth operation of payment systems and to provide services to the EU institutions and other public bodies.

3. Bank of Japan

The Bank of Japan (BOJ) is the central bank of Japan and is responsible for the country's monetary policy. The bank was established in 1882 and is headquartered in Tokyo. The main objective of the BOJ is to maintain price stability, which means keeping inflation low and stable. The BOJ uses a variety of tools to achieve this goal, including setting interest rates, buying and selling government bonds, and providing financial assistance to financial institutions.

The BOJ's monetary policy decisions are made by the Policy Board, which is made up of the Governor and six other members. The Governor of the BOJ is appointed by the Japanese government and serves a five-year term.

The BOJ also plays a role in the stability of the financial system, it monitors the financial system, and conducts research on financial and economic issues. It also has supervisory responsibilities for the banking sector in Japan.

In addition to its monetary policy and financial stability functions, the BOJ also acts as the fiscal agent for the Japanese government, manages its foreign exchange reserves, and provides banking services to the government and other public bodies.

BOJ has been implementing a monetary policy framework called "Quantitative and Qualitative Monetary Easing (QQE)" since 2013, which aims to achieve the price stability target of 2% inflation, by controlling the money supply and interest rate.

B. GENERAL FUNCTIONS OF CENTRAL BANK:

The main functions of a central bank are common all over the world. But the scope and content of policy objectives may vary from country to country and from period to period depending on the economic situations of the respective country.

Generally, all the central banks aim at achieving economic stability along with a high growth rate and a favorable external payment position through proper monetary management. The common functions of central banks are discussed below.

1.Regulator of currency

The issue of paper money is one of the most important functions of a central bank. As the sole authority to issue currency for circulation, the central bank ensures that the money in circulation is legal tender. The issue department of the central bank is responsible for issuing notes and coins to commercial banks, facilitating the distribution of currency throughout the economy. Additionally, the central bank regulates the credit and currency supply based on the economic situation of the country, adjusting monetary policies to maintain stability.

In terms of currency issuance, the central bank is required to hold a certain amount or a fixed proportion of gold and foreign securities against the total notes issued. This practice ensures that the currency in circulation is backed by tangible assets, promoting confidence in the financial system. Specifically, the Reserve Bank of India (RBI) is required to maintain Gold and Foreign Exchange Reserves worth Rs. 200 Crore, of which at least Rs. 115 Crore must be in gold. This is known as the Minimum Reserve System, a framework that continues to this day.

By having a monopoly over the issuance of currency, the central bank gains several advantages. Firstly, it ensures uniformity in the notes issued and allows for effective control over the money supply. This contributes to greater stability in the monetary system and builds public confidence in the currency. Moreover, the government benefits financially by earning profits from the printing of currency. Thus, the central bank's exclusive authority over currency issuance not only fosters economic stability but also serves as a source of revenue for the government.

2. Banker, agent and adviser to the government

The central bank of a country plays a crucial role by acting as the banker, fiscal agent, and advisor to the government. In its capacity as a banker, the central bank holds the deposits of both central and state governments and processes payments on their behalf. This ensures smooth management of government funds and financial transactions. Additionally, the central bank is responsible for buying and selling foreign currencies on behalf of the government, facilitating international trade and monetary policies. It also maintains the country's stock of gold, contributing to the security of the national reserves.

As a fiscal agent, the central bank provides short-term loans to the government, typically for periods not exceeding 90 days, helping to meet temporary funding requirements. It also floats loans and provides advances to state governments and local bodies, ensuring they have access to necessary financial resources for development projects. Beyond short-term loans, the central bank manages the entire public debt on behalf of the government, handling the issuance, servicing, and repayment of government debt instruments.

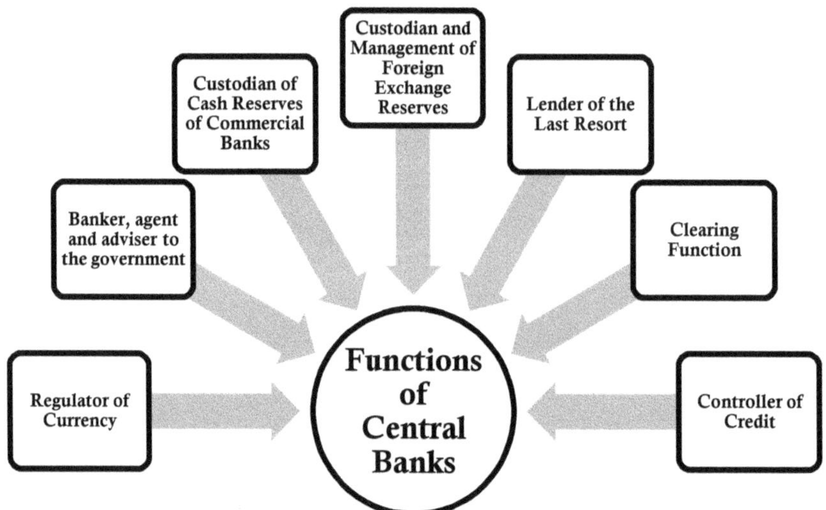

Exhibit 1.1: Functions of Central Banks

In its advisory role, the central bank offers valuable guidance to the government on significant monetary and economic issues. This includes advice on matters such as currency devaluation, foreign exchange policy, and budgetary policies. By performing these roles, the central bank not only supports the government's financial operations but also contributes to the overall economic stability of the country.

3. Custodian of cash reserves of commercial banks

Commercial banks are mandated to maintain a certain percentage of their cash reserves with the central bank. This requirement ensures that banks have adequate liquidity and serves as a safeguard against financial instability. By holding these reserves, the central bank has oversight of the commercial banks' liquidity, which helps in regulating the money supply and maintaining overall financial discipline within the banking system.

Based on these reserves, the central bank facilitates the transfer of funds between banks to ensure the smooth clearing of cheques. When banks process cheque transactions, the central bank acts as an intermediary, transferring the necessary funds from one bank's reserve to another. This system helps streamline interbank payments, ensuring that cheque clearance is efficient and that the banking system functions without disruptions. The central bank's role in managing reserves and facilitating these transactions plays a critical part in maintaining the liquidity and operational stability of the entire banking sector.

4. Custodian and management of foreign exchange reserves

The central bank is responsible for managing and safeguarding the foreign exchange reserves of a country. These reserves consist of foreign currencies, gold, and other international assets, which the central bank holds to ensure the country's ability to meet its international payment obligations. By maintaining an adequate level of foreign reserves, the central bank can help stabilize the economy during times of external financial shocks or currency volatility.

One of the central bank's key functions is to fix the exchange rate of the domestic currency in relation to foreign currencies. This involves determining the value of the national currency in the global market, ensuring it remains competitive and stable. In cases where exchange rates fluctuate due to external factors, the central bank steps in to minimize instability. It achieves this by actively buying or selling foreign currencies in the market to prevent excessive fluctuations. By doing so, the central bank maintains stability in foreign exchange rates, which is essential for fostering international trade, investment, and overall economic confidence.

5. Lender of the last resort

The central bank functions as the lender of last resort by providing financial accommodation to commercial banks, bill brokers, and other financial institutions through re-discounts and collateral advances. In times of liquidity crises or financial distress, when these institutions are unable to secure funds from other sources, the central bank steps in to offer financial support. This ensures that financial institutions have access to necessary funds to meet their obligations, thereby preventing a potential liquidity crunch.

The central bank lends to these institutions specifically to help them during difficult situations, such as a shortage of cash or unexpected withdrawals. By offering loans and advances, the central bank safeguards the broader financial system from potential collapse. This role is critical in maintaining trust and stability in the banking system, as it assures that banks can rely on the central bank for support in times of financial stress, ultimately preserving the integrity of the country's financial structure.

6. Clearing function

The central bank performs the crucial function of acting as a clearing house for other banks, facilitating the settlement of mutual obligations between them. In its role as a clearing house, the central bank helps streamline interbank transactions by enabling the transfer of funds, ensuring that payments between banks are settled efficiently and smoothly. Since the central bank holds the cash reserves of commercial banks, it is uniquely positioned to perform this role, making the settlement process more straightforward and reliable.

The clearing house system deals with the clearance and settlement of various paper-based instruments such as cheques, drafts, payment orders, interest or dividend warrants, and more. These instruments are processed, and the amounts owed between different banks are calculated and settled, ensuring that transactions are completed securely and accurately.

A clearing house acts as an intermediary that facilitates the exchange of obligations between two parties in a transaction, particularly in financial dealings. It serves as a neutral third party to match and confirm trade details, set financial obligations, and ensure that all parties involved in the transaction adhere to the terms of their agreement. This role is vital in maintaining trust and efficiency in financial markets and banking systems, as it reduces the risks associated with direct transactions between parties.

7. Controller of credit:

One of the most significant functions of the central bank is to control the credit creation ability of commercial banks, which is essential for managing inflationary and deflationary pressures within the economy. By regulating the amount of credit that banks can extend to businesses and consumers, the central bank helps maintain economic stability. This control over credit is critical in preventing excessive money supply during inflationary periods and ensuring adequate credit flow during deflationary phases.

To achieve this, the central bank employs both Quantitative and Qualitative (Selective) methods. Quantitative methods focus on controlling the overall cost and quantity of credit in the economy.

These methods include:

a) Bank rate policy:
The central bank adjusts the interest rate at which it lends to commercial banks. By increasing or decreasing the bank rate, it influences the interest rates that commercial banks charge their customers, thereby affecting borrowing and lending behavior.

b) Open market operations:
The central bank buys or sells government securities in the open market to regulate the money supply. When it sells securities, it absorbs money from the economy, reducing liquidity. Conversely, when it buys securities, it injects money into the system, increasing liquidity.

c) Variations in reserve ratios:
The central bank changes the reserve requirements for commercial banks, dictating the proportion of deposits that banks must keep in reserve and not lend out. By raising the reserve ratio, the central bank can limit the amount of credit available, while lowering it can boost lending capacity.

These methods collectively allow the central bank to manage credit creation and ensure the stability of the financial system.

C. RESERVE BANK OF INDIA

The Reserve Bank of India is the central bank of the country, Central banks are a relatively recent innovation and most central banks, as we know them today, were established around the early twentieth century.

The Reserve Bank of India was set up on the basis of the recommendations of the Hilton Young Commission. The Reserve Bank of India Act, 1934 (II of 1934) provides the statutory basis of the functioning of the bank, which commenced operations on April 1, 1935.

The Reserve Bank of India (RBI) began its operations by taking over key functions from other institutions. It assumed the role previously performed by the Controller of Currency, which was responsible for the issuance and regulation of currency in the country. Additionally, it took over the management of Government accounts and public debt from the Imperial Bank of India, streamlining the government's financial operations under a centralized authority

After the partition of India, the RBI, originally established as a shareholder's bank, underwent a significant transformation when it was nationalized in 1949. This marked a new chapter in its history, positioning it as a public institution responsible for the nation's monetary stability and financial governance.

At its inception, the RBI played a special role in fostering development, particularly in the area of agriculture. This developmental focus distinguished it from other central banks, as it contributed significantly to agricultural financing and rural development in India.

With the liberalization of the Indian economy, the RBI's focus shifted back to its core central banking functions, which include formulating Monetary Policy, ensuring Bank Supervision and Regulation, and Overseeing the Payment System. In addition, the bank now plays a crucial role in developing financial markets to ensure stability and growth.

The RBI also oversees four key subsidiaries that extend its influence in various sectors. These subsidiaries include the National Housing Bank (NHB), which focuses on housing finance, the National Bank for Agriculture and Rural Development (NABARD), which supports rural development, the Deposit Insurance and Credit Guarantee Corporation of India (DICGC), which insures deposits, and the Bharatiya Reserve Bank Note Mudran Private Limited (BRBNMPL), responsible for printing currency notes.

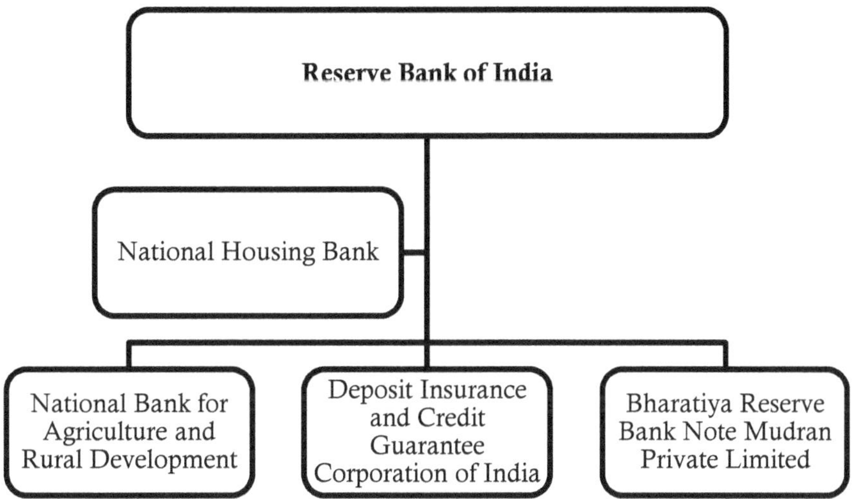

Exhibit 1.2: Subsidaries of Reserve Bank of India

The Bank was constituted to:

i. Regulate the issue of banknotes

ii. Maintain reserves to secure monetary stability and

iii. To operate the credit and currency system of the country to its advantage.

D.Functions of central bank with reference to RBI

The Reserve Bank of India (RBI) is the central bank of India and is responsible for the country's monetary policy. The bank was established in 1935 and is headquartered in Mumbai.

The main functions of the RBI are:

1. Monetary Policy:

The RBI employs various tools like adjusting interest rates and engaging in open market operations to regulate the money supply in the economy. This helps the RBI achieve its goal of maintaining a target inflation rate while promoting economic growth and stability.

2. Financial Stability:

The RBI is responsible for ensuring the stability of India's financial system. It monitors economic trends and the banking sector, taking necessary measures to maintain financial soundness. This includes oversight of systemic risks and ensuring that financial institutions adhere to regulations.

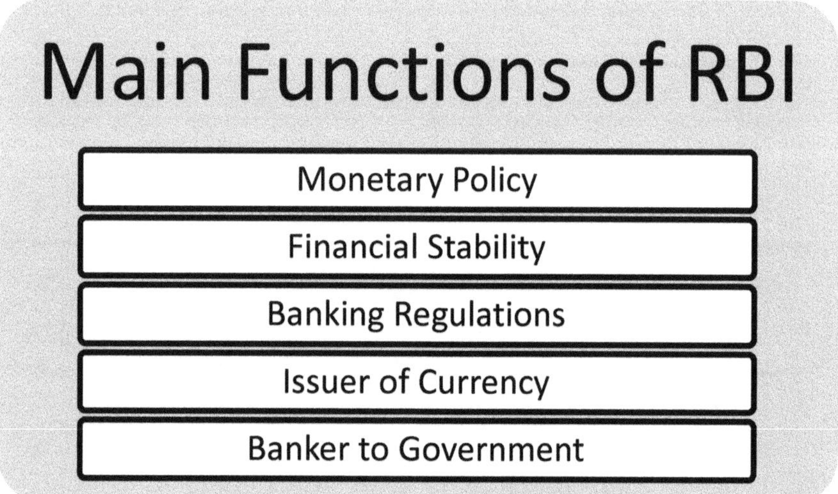

Exhibit 1.3: Main Functions of RBI

3. Banking Regulation:

As a regulatory authority, the RBI issues licenses to banks and other financial institutions. It ensures that these entities comply with established banking regulations and supervisory guidelines aimed at maintaining the integrity of the financial system.

4. Issuer of Currency:

The RBI has the exclusive right to issue and manage the currency in India. It oversees the design, printing, and distribution of banknotes to ensure adequate supply and proper circulation of legal tender in the economy.

5. Banker to the Government:

The RBI functions as the government's banker, managing its accounts and transactions. This includes facilitating the collection of taxes, making payments, and managing public debt on behalf of both the central and state governments.

These key roles illustrate the multifaceted responsibilities of the RBI in regulating monetary policy, ensuring financial stability, and managing banking operations and currency in India.

E. `Traditional functions of RBI

1. Issue of Currency Notes

The Reserve Bank of India (RBI) holds the sole authority or monopoly on issuing currency notes in India, with the exception of the one-rupee note and smaller denomination coins, which are issued by the Government of India. This exclusive right allows the RBI to manage the country's currency circulation effectively, ensuring monetary stability.

The currency notes issued by the RBI are considered legal tender, meaning they must be accepted for all payments within the country. These notes are currently issued in denominations of Rs. 5, 10, 20, 50, 100, 500, and 1,000, and are widely used for transactions across India.

In addition to issuing currency, the RBI has the authority to withdraw notes from circulation and even exchange them for other denominations, allowing it to manage the liquidity and flow of money in the economy as needed. The issuance of these currency notes is backed by a reserve of assets to maintain their value. The RBI issues notes against the security of assets such as gold bullion, foreign securities, rupee coins, exchange bills, promissory notes, and Government of India bonds. This ensures the stability and trustworthiness of the currency in circulation.

2. Banker to other Banks

As the apex monetary institution, the Reserve Bank of India (RBI) possesses obligatory powers to guide, assist, and direct commercial banks across the country. This supervisory role ensures that commercial banks operate within a framework of regulatory guidelines and standards, promoting financial stability and effective banking practice

Traditional Functions	Developmental / Promotional Functions of RBI	Supervisory Functions of RBI
• Issue of Currency Notes • Banker to other Banks • Banker to the Government • Exchange Rate Management • Credit Control Function • Supervisory Function	• Development of the Financial System • Development of Agriculture • Provision of Industrial Finance • Provisions of Training • Collection of Data • Publication of the Reports • Promotion of Banking Habits • Promotion of Export through Refinance	• Granting license to banks • Bank Inspection • Control over NBFIs • Implementation of the Deposit Insurance Scheme

Exhibit 1.4: Specific functions of RBI

The RBI has the authority to control the volumes of bank reserves, influencing how much credit commercial banks can create. By adjusting reserve requirements, the RBI can directly impact the lending capacity of banks, ensuring that credit creation aligns with the broader economic goals and stability measures.

Every commercial bank is required to maintain a portion of their reserves with the RBI. This practice helps in the centralization of reserves, enhancing the RBI's ability to monitor and manage the liquidity of the banking system effectively.

In times of financial need or urgency, commercial banks can approach the RBI for funds. This facility is crucial for maintaining stability during liquidity shortages or financial stress. Consequently, the RBI is often referred to as the lender of last resort, reflecting its role in providing emergency financial support to banks to prevent systemic crises and uphold the integrity of the financial system.

3. Banker to the Government

As the apex monetary authority, the Reserve Bank of India (RBI) serves as an essential agent for both the central and state governments. This role encompasses a range of banking functions crucial for effective governmental financial management.

The RBI performs several banking functions on behalf of the government, including accepting deposits, handling tax collections, and making payments. These activities facilitate the smooth operation of government financial transactions and support the overall fiscal management of the country.

At the international level, the RBI represents the government in various financial and economic forums. This role includes engaging with international institutions and participating in global financial discussions, ensuring that India's interests are effectively represented and managed.

The RBI is also responsible for maintaining government accounts and providing financial advice to the government. This advisory role is critical in shaping fiscal policies and making informed decisions regarding national economic strategies.

Additionally, the RBI manages government public debts and maintains foreign exchange reserves on behalf of the government. This management includes handling the issuance and servicing of government debt, as well as managing reserves to stabilize the country's currency and ensure financial stability.

In times of financial need, the RBI provides an overdraft facility to the government, allowing it to address short-term financial shortfalls. This facility ensures that the government can continue its operations and meet its financial obligations even during periods of financial crunch.

4. Exchange Rate Management

Maintaining the stability of the external value of the rupee is a crucial function of the Reserve Bank of India (RBI). This responsibility involves crafting and implementing domestic policies aimed at ensuring that the rupee remains stable and resilient in the face of external economic pressures. The RBI's policies are designed to support the rupee's value and manage its fluctuations in international markets.

To achieve exchange rate stability, the RBI must develop and execute a comprehensive foreign exchange rate policy. This policy includes various measures and interventions to stabilize the value of the rupee against other currencies, particularly the U.S. Dollar. Effective implementation of this policy helps to manage exchange rate volatility and ensures a more predictable environment for international trade and investment.

A key aspect of maintaining exchange rate stability involves balancing the demand and supply of foreign currency. The RBI works to bring the demand for foreign currencies, such as the U.S. Dollar, into alignment with their supply. By intervening in the foreign exchange market, the RBI can influence exchange rates and manage currency reserves, thus contributing to overall economic stability and reducing the risk of excessive currency fluctuations.

F. Development or Promotional functions of RBI

Developmental Functions of RBI	
	Developemt of Financial System
	Development of Agriculture
	Provision of Industrial Finance
	Provisions of Training
	Collection of Data
	Promotion of Banking Habits
	Promotion of Export through Refinance
	Publication of the Reports

Exhibit 1.5: Development Functions of RBI

1. Development of the Financial System

The financial system encompasses a broad network of components, including financial institutions, financial markets, and financial instruments. This system is crucial for the functioning of an economy, facilitating the flow of funds between savers and borrowers and supporting various economic activities.

A sound and efficient financial system is essential for the rapid economic development of a nation. It ensures that resources are allocated effectively, risks are managed prudently, and financial stability is maintained. Such a system supports economic growth by providing businesses with access to capital, consumers with credit, and governments with the ability to implement fiscal policies.

To support and enhance the financial system, the Reserve Bank of India (RBI) has actively encouraged the establishment of both banking and non-banking financial institutions. These institutions cater to the diverse credit needs of various sectors within the economy, from agriculture and small businesses to large enterprises. By fostering a diverse range of financial institutions, the RBI helps ensure that the credit requirements of different sectors are met, promoting balanced economic growth and stability.

2. Development of Agriculture

In an agrarian economy such as India's, the Reserve Bank of India (RBI) plays a crucial role in addressing the credit needs of agriculture and related activities. Given the significant reliance on agriculture for livelihoods and economic stability, the RBI has implemented various measures to ensure that the sector receives adequate financial support.

The RBI has been successful in increasing the flow of credit to agriculture and allied sectors, thereby supporting the growth and development of this vital part of the economy. Through targeted policies and initiatives, the RBI has worked to enhance the availability of funds for agricultural activities, which is essential for improving productivity and ensuring the sector's sustainability.

Historically, the RBI established institutions such as the Agriculture Refinance and Development Corporation (ARDC) to manage agricultural credit. Although the ARDC was later absorbed into the National Bank for Agriculture and Rural Development (NABARD), it laid the groundwork for systematic agricultural financing. Today, NABARD, along with Regional Rural Banks (RRBs), continues to play a pivotal role in managing and disbursing credit to the rural and agricultural sectors. These institutions are integral to the RBI's strategy for promoting agricultural development and rural financial inclusion.

3. Provision of Industrial Finance

Rapid industrial growth is fundamental to achieving faster economic development, as it drives innovation, creates jobs, and boosts overall productivity. To support this growth, the availability of adequate and timely credit to industries of all sizes—small, medium, and large—is crucial. Access to financial resources enables businesses to expand operations, invest in new technologies, and compete effectively in the market.

The Reserve Bank of India (RBI) has played a key role in facilitating industrial development by establishing and supporting various special financial institutions. These institutions are designed to cater to the diverse credit needs of industries and to promote industrial growth across different sectors. For instance, the RBI's initiatives led to the creation of institutions such as ICICI Ltd., which provides a range of financial services and credit facilities to businesses. Similarly, the Industrial Development Bank of India (IDBI) was set up to provide long-term finance to industries, while the Small Industries Development Bank of India (SIDBI) focuses on supporting small and medium enterprises. Additionally, the Export-Import Bank of India (EXIM Bank) plays a crucial role in financing international trade, thereby supporting industrial exports. Through these institutions, the RBI has effectively contributed to the industrialization and economic progress of the country.

4. Provisions of Training

The Reserve Bank of India (RBI) has consistently prioritized the provision of essential training to the staff of the banking industry. Recognizing that skilled and knowledgeable personnel are vital for the effective functioning of the financial sector, the RBI has established various initiatives to enhance the capabilities of banking professionals.

To support this goal, the RBI has set up bankers' training colleges in several locations across the country. These institutions are dedicated to providing comprehensive training programs that cover a wide range of banking and financial topics, ensuring that staff are well-equipped to handle their roles efficiently.

Among the notable training institutions are the National Institute of Bank Management (NIBM), which offers advanced management training and research in banking; the Bankers Staff College (BSC), which focuses on the professional development of bank staff; and the College of Agricultural Banking (CAB), which specializes in training related to agricultural banking. These institutions play a crucial role in enhancing the skill sets of banking professionals, thus contributing to the overall efficiency and effectiveness of the banking sector.

5. Collection of Data

As the apex monetary authority of the country, the Reserve Bank of India (RBI) undertakes the important task of collecting, processing, and disseminating statistical data on a wide range of topics. This responsibility is central to the RBI's role in monitoring and analyzing economic trends, as well as in formulating and implementing monetary policy.

The RBI's data collection efforts encompass various critical areas, including interest rates, inflation, savings, and investments. By systematically gathering and analyzing this data, the RBI provides valuable insights that are essential for understanding economic conditions and trends.

This statistical data is not only crucial for the RBI's internal decision-making processes but also serves as a valuable resource for researchers and policy makers. Access to accurate and comprehensive data allows these stakeholders to make informed decisions, develop effective policies, and contribute to the overall economic stability and growth of the country.

6. Promotion of Banking Habits

As the apex financial institution in India, the Reserve Bank of India (RBI) plays a pivotal role in promoting banking habits across the country. Recognizing the importance of widespread banking participation for economic stability and growth, the RBI undertakes various initiatives to encourage individuals to engage with formal banking systems.

The RBI actively works to institutionalize savings by implementing measures aimed at expanding the banking network. By fostering a culture of saving and financial inclusion, the RBI helps ensure that more people have access to banking services and are encouraged to manage their finances through formal channels.

To support this goal, the RBI has established several key institutions over the years. These include the Deposit Insurance Corporation (1962), which provides insurance for deposits to enhance public confidence in the banking system; the Unit Trust of India (UTI) (1964), which promotes investment and savings; the Industrial Development Bank of India (IDBI) (1964), which supports industrial financing; the National Bank for Agriculture and Rural Development (NABARD) (1982), which focuses on agricultural and rural development; and the National Housing Bank (NHB) (1988), which promotes housing finance.

These organizations contribute significantly to developing and promoting banking habits among the populace. Additionally, during economic reforms, the RBI has introduced various initiatives to further encourage and support banking activities in India, thereby enhancing financial literacy and inclusion throughout the country.

7. Promotion of Export through Refinance

The Reserve Bank of India (RBI) plays a crucial role in promoting exports by facilitating financial support for foreign trade. As part of its commitment to enhancing India's export activities, the RBI provides various mechanisms to encourage and support financing for exports.

One of the key ways the RBI supports export financing is through refinancing. This process involves the RBI offering refinancing facilities to financial institutions that provide loans for export purposes. By doing so, the RBI ensures that commercial banks and other financial entities have the necessary resources to extend credit to exporters, thereby stimulating international trade.

To further bolster export activities, the RBI supports two significant institutions: the Export-Import Bank of India (EXIM Bank) and the Export Credit Guarantee Corporation of India (ECGC). The EXIM Bank plays a vital role in providing financial assistance for export activities, including short-term and long-term credit facilities. Similarly, the ECGC offers credit insurance and guarantees to protect exporters against potential losses from non-payment by foreign buyers. The RBI's refinancing support to these institutions enhances their ability to offer competitive and comprehensive financial products to exporters, thereby promoting and facilitating India's export growth.

8. Publication of the Reports

The Reserve Bank of India (RBI) maintains a dedicated publication division responsible for collecting, analyzing, and disseminating data on various sectors of the economy. This division plays a crucial role in ensuring that valuable economic and financial information is systematically organized and made accessible to the public.

The RBI regularly publishes a range of reports and bulletins that provide comprehensive insights into the state of the economy, financial sector performance, and other relevant economic indicators. Key publications include the RBI Weekly Reports, which offer updates on recent developments and activities; the RBI Annual Report, which presents a detailed overview of the Bank's operations, financial health, and key achievements over the year; and the Report on Trend and Progress of Commercial Banks in India, which reviews the performance and trends within the banking sector.

These reports and bulletins are made available to the public at affordable rates, ensuring that stakeholders, including researchers, policymakers, and the general public, have access to essential data and analyses. By providing this information, the RBI supports transparency and informed decision-making, contributing to a better understanding of economic and financial conditions in India.

G. Supervisory functions of RBI

1. Granting license to banks

The Reserve Bank of India (RBI) plays a pivotal role in the regulation and supervision of the banking sector through the process of granting licenses to banks. This function is crucial for maintaining the stability and integrity of the financial system.

Firstly, the RBI grants licenses to banks to operate and conduct banking business within India. This licensing process ensures that only those institutions that meet the prescribed criteria and standards are authorized to provide banking services. By regulating the entry of new banks, the RBI helps to ensure that the sector remains sound and competitive.

In addition to initial licensing, the RBI is also responsible for granting permissions for opening extension counters and new branches. This facilitates the expansion of banking services to underserved or emerging areas, thereby enhancing financial inclusion and accessibility. Conversely, the RBI also oversees the process for closing down existing branches, ensuring that such decisions are made in a controlled and orderly manner.

This regulatory oversight helps to prevent any potential disruptions in banking services and maintains the overall stability of the banking infrastructure.

2. Bank Inspection

The Reserve Bank of India (RBI) is deeply involved in ensuring the soundness and stability of the banking sector through rigorous bank inspection processes. This function is essential for maintaining the financial health of banks and protecting depositors' interests.

To start with, the RBI grants licenses to banks that operate in accordance with its directives and demonstrate prudent management practices. The central bank ensures that banks adhere to regulatory standards and avoid engaging in undue risks that could jeopardize their stability. This careful scrutiny before granting licenses helps in fostering a robust and resilient banking environment.

Supervisory Functions of RBI

| Granting License to Banks | Bank Inspection | Control over NBFIs | Implementation of the Deposit Insurance Scheme |

Exhibit 1.6: Supervisory Functions of RBI

Furthermore, the RBI has the authority to request periodical information from banks regarding various aspects of their financial health, including components of assets and liabilities. This regular reporting requirement allows the RBI to monitor banks' performance, assess their risk exposures, and ensure compliance with regulatory norms. By analyzing this information, the RBI can detect any potential issues early and take corrective measures, if necessary, thereby safeguarding the overall integrity of the banking system.

3. Control over NBFIs

The Reserve Bank of India (RBI) exercises control over Non-Banking Financial Institutions (NBFIs) to ensure their sound operation and stability within the financial system, despite NBFIs not being directly influenced by monetary policy.

Firstly, NBFIs are not directly impacted by monetary policy in the same manner as commercial banks. This means that their operations are not automatically aligned with the central bank's policy measures designed to manage the economy's money supply and interest rates. However, to maintain systemic stability, the RBI retains the authority to issue directives to NBFIs. These directives are aimed at guiding the operations and practices of NBFIs, ensuring they adhere to prudent standards and regulatory requirements.

Additionally, the RBI performs periodic inspections of NBFIs to monitor their financial health and compliance with regulations. These inspections allow the RBI to assess the risk exposures, operational practices, and overall stability of NBFIs. By conducting these evaluations, the RBI can enforce necessary corrections and ensure that NBFIs contribute positively to the financial ecosystem while safeguarding against potential risks that could affect the broader economy.

4. Implementation of the Deposit Insurance Scheme

The Reserve Bank of India (RBI) exercises control over Non-Banking Financial Institutions (NBFIs) to ensure their sound operation and stability within the financial system, despite NBFIs not being directly influenced by monetary policy.

Firstly, NBFIs are not directly impacted by monetary policy in the same manner as commercial banks. This means that their operations are not automatically aligned with the central bank's policy measures designed to manage the economy's money supply and interest rates. However, to maintain systemic stability, the RBI retains the authority to issue directives to NBFIs. These directives are aimed at guiding the operations and practices of NBFIs, ensuring they adhere to prudent standards and regulatory requirements.

Additionally, the RBI performs periodic inspections of NBFIs to monitor their financial health and compliance with regulations. These inspections allow the RBI to assess the risk exposures, operational practices, and overall stability of NBFIs. By conducting these evaluations, the RBI can enforce necessary corrections and ensure that NBFIs contribute positively to the financial ecosystem while safeguarding against potential risks that could affect the broader economy.

H. Objectives of RBI

Some of the main objectives of RBI include the following:
1. Primary objectives
According to the Reserve Bank of India Act, 1934, the primary objectives of the Reserve Bank of India (RBI) are foundational to its role as the central bank and pivotal to maintaining the economic stability of the country.

One of the foremost objectives is to govern the issue of bank notes. The RBI holds the exclusive authority to issue currency notes, ensuring that the money supply in the economy is controlled and regulated. This function is essential for maintaining the credibility and stability of the currency.

Another key objective is to maintain reserves to ensure monetary stability. The RBI manages and holds reserves of gold, foreign exchange, and other assets to safeguard the value of the rupee and support the stability of the country's financial system. These reserves are crucial for managing inflation, supporting the currency, and addressing any external economic shocks.

The RBI is also tasked with running the currency and credit systems of the nation to promote economic growth and financial stability. This includes overseeing the supply of money and credit to ensure they meet the needs of the economy while avoiding inflationary or deflationary pressures.

Furthermore, the RBI aims to operate free from political influence. This independence is vital for the central bank to conduct monetary policy effectively and make decisions based on economic rather than political considerations. By maintaining this autonomy, the RBI can focus on its core mandate of ensuring financial stability and supporting economic development without undue external pressures.

2. Fundamental objectives
The fundamental objectives of the Reserve Bank of India (RBI) center around its central banking functions within the Indian financial

market. These objectives are crucial for the stability and efficiency of the country's monetary system and financial infrastructure.

Firstly, the RBI serves as the banker's bank. In this capacity, it acts as the primary banking institution for other banks operating within India. The RBI provides essential services such as clearing and settlement of inter-bank transactions, managing the reserve requirements of commercial banks, and offering emergency funding to maintain liquidity and stability in the banking sector.

Secondly, the RBI holds the role of note-issuing authority. It has the exclusive right to issue and manage currency notes in India. This function involves regulating the supply of money to ensure that it aligns with the economic needs of the country, maintaining the trust and value of the currency, and managing the issuance and withdrawal of currency notes to prevent counterfeiting and ensure smooth transactions.

Lastly, the RBI acts as the banker to the government. This involves managing the financial operations of both the central and state governments. The RBI is responsible for maintaining government accounts, facilitating government transactions, managing public debt, and advising on financial and monetary policy. This role is integral to ensuring that government finances are effectively managed and aligned with broader economic goals.

These fundamental objectives underscore the RBI's pivotal role in maintaining financial stability, regulating the money supply, and supporting the overall economic framework of India.

3. Encourage growth

The fundamental objectives of the Reserve Bank of India (RBI) center around its central banking functions within the Indian financial market. These objectives are crucial for the stability and efficiency of the country's monetary system and financial infrastructure.

Firstly, the RBI serves as the banker's bank. In this capacity, it acts as the primary banking institution for other banks operating within India. The RBI provides essential services such as clearing and settlement of inter-bank transactions, managing the reserve requirements of commercial banks, and offering emergency funding to maintain liquidity and stability in the banking sector.

Secondly, the RBI holds the role of note-issuing authority. It has the exclusive right to issue and manage currency notes in India. This function involves regulating the supply of money to ensure that it aligns with the economic needs of the country, maintaining the trust and value of the currency, and managing the issuance and withdrawal of currency notes to prevent counterfeiting and ensure smooth transactions.

Lastly, the RBI acts as the banker to the government. This involves managing the financial operations of both the central and state governments. The RBI is responsible for maintaining government accounts, facilitating government transactions, managing public debt, and advising on financial and monetary policy. This role is integral to ensuring that 27overnmentt finances are effectively managed and aligned with broader economic goals.

4. Advancement of the economy of India

A major objective of the Reserve Bank of India (RBI) is to support the planned advancement of India's economy. This objective extends beyond the traditional central banking functions, encompassing a broader role in promoting economic development and growth.

Historically, the RBI's role was primarily focused on regulating monetary policy, managing currency, and overseeing the financial stability of the banking sector. However, with the introduction of five-year plans and broader economic development programs, the RBI has adapted its approach to include a range of developmental and promotional activities. In alignment with the nation's economic planning, the RBI engages in various initiatives that aim to foster economic growth, support industrialization, and improve agricultural productivity. This involves implementing policies and programs that provide financial support to key sectors, such as agriculture, small and medium-sized enterprises (SMEs), and infrastructure development.

The RBI's commitment to economic advancement includes facilitating access to credit, promoting financial inclusion, and supporting the establishment of financial institutions that cater to diverse economic needs. By doing so, the RBI helps drive economic development and contributes to the overall advancement of the Indian economy, ensuring that its monetary and financial policies are effectively integrated with national development objectives.

Overall, the main emphasis of the RBI is to monitor and make rules and regulations for the financial sector that includes financial organisations, commercial banks, and non-banking financial organisations. Some comprehensive and important influences of the RBI are to restructure the bank inspection process and stimulate the auditor's role in the banking sector.

I. COMMERCIAL BANK

A commercial bank is a financial institution that provides a variety of services to individuals and businesses, including accepting deposits, making loans, and offering basic investment products. Commercial banks are profit-oriented and aim to generate revenue by lending money and investing in financial markets.

Some of the key services offered by commercial banks include:
1. Checking and Savings Accounts:
Commercial banks provide a variety of deposit accounts, including checking and savings accounts, tailored to meet the needs of both individuals and businesses. These accounts allow customers to securely deposit, withdraw, and manage their money.

2. Loans:
Commercial banks offer a range of loan products, such as personal loans, auto loans, mortgages, and business loans. These loans help individuals and businesses finance various needs, from purchasing a home or car to expanding a business.

3. Credit Cards:
Commercial banks issue credit cards, enabling customers to make purchases on credit. These cards offer convenience and often come

with benefits like rewards, but they also require responsible management to avoid debt accumulation.

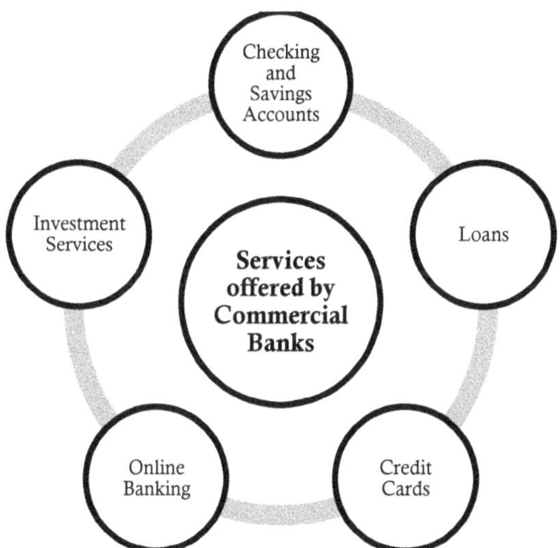

Exhibit 1.7: Services Offered by Commercial Banks

4. Online Banking:

With the advancement of technology, commercial banks offer online banking services. These services allow customers to manage their accounts, make payments, transfer funds, and monitor transactions electronically, providing convenience and efficiency.

5. Investment Services:

Commercial banks offer basic investment options such as certificates of deposit (CDs), money market accounts, and mutual funds. These investment products provide customers with opportunities to grow their savings over time.

In addition to providing these essential banking services, commercial banks play a crucial role in the economy by offering credit to individuals and businesses. This access to credit supports capital projects, economic growth, and development, while also ensuring that the general public has access to fundamental financial services.

J. IMPORTANCE OF COMMERCIAL BANKS IN INDIA

Commercial banks play a crucial role in the Indian economy and have a significant impact on the financial system and the overall growth of the country.

Some of the key importance of commercial banks in India are:
1. Financial intermediation:
Commercial banks act as intermediaries between savers and borrowers, facilitating the flow of funds from savers to borrowers and thereby promoting economic growth.

2. Access to credit:
Commercial banks play an important role in providing access to credit, particularly to small and medium-sized enterprises (SMEs) and low-income households that may not have access to other sources of financing.

3. Financial inclusion:
Commercial banks are instrumental in promoting financial inclusion by providing basic banking services, such as savings accounts, to a larger segment of the population, including rural and unbanked areas.

4. Stabilization of the economy:
Commercial banks help stabilize the economy by providing a steady flow of credit and maintaining the stability of the financial system.

5. Support for government initiatives:
Commercial banks play a key role in supporting government initiatives, such as schemes aimed at promoting entrepreneurship, providing affordable housing, and promoting financial literacy.

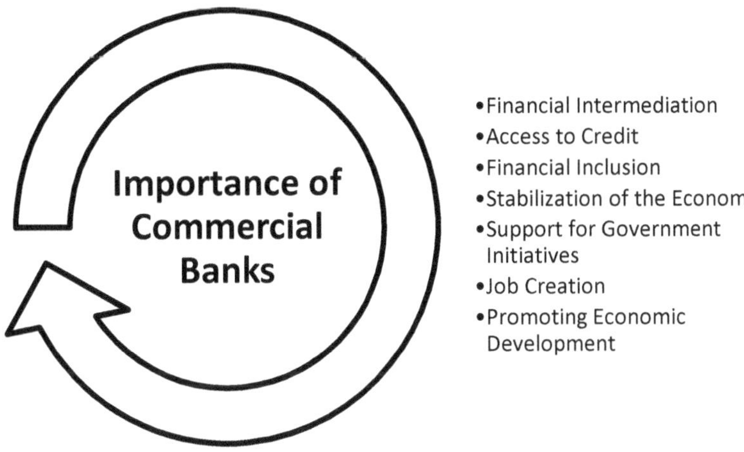

Exhibit 1.8: Importance of Commercial Banks

6. Job creation:

Commercial banks create employment opportunities directly, through the creation of branches and other offices, and indirectly, by promoting economic growth and entrepreneurship.

7. Promoting economic development:

Commercial banks play a critical role in promoting economic development by financing capital projects, supporting small and medium-sized enterprises, and providing access to credit for low-income households.

In conclusion, commercial banks are essential for the development of the Indian economy and play a vital role in promoting financial stability, fostering economic growth, and promoting financial inclusion.

K. FUNCTIONS OF COMMERCIAL BANKS

Commercial banks are financial institutions that provide a variety of services to individuals and businesses.

The main functions of commercial banks are:
1. Accepting Deposits:

One of the fundamental roles of commercial banks is to accept deposits from customers. They offer a variety of deposit accounts, such as savings accounts, checking accounts, and certificates of deposit (CDs). These accounts provide customers with a safe place to store their money while earning interest in the case of savings accounts and CDs. By collecting deposits, banks accumulate the capital needed to provide loans and other financial services.

2. Providing Loans:

To generate additional income, commercial banks invest a portion of the funds they hold from deposits in various financial markets. Banks typically invest in low-risk financial instruments like government bonds, corporate bonds, and securities. By engaging in these investments, banks ensure they are not solely reliant on loan interest for income but also diversify their income streams

3. Investing:

To generate additional income, commercial banks invest a portion of the funds they hold from deposits in various financial markets. Banks typically invest in low-risk financial instruments like government bonds, corporate bonds, and securities. By engaging in these investments, banks ensure they are not solely reliant on loan interest for income but also diversify their income streams

4. Payment Services:

Commercial banks provide a variety of payment services to facilitate the smooth transfer of funds. This includes processing checks, conducting wire transfers, and offering electronic payment systems such as online banking and mobile payment apps. These services are essential for businesses and individuals alike, ensuring secure and efficient methods for conducting both domestic and international transactions.

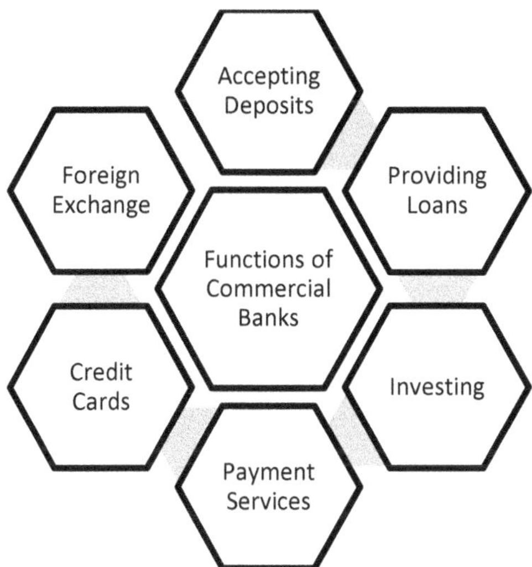

Exhibit 1.9: Functions of Commercial Banks

5. Credit Cards:

Many commercial banks issue credit cards, allowing their customers to make purchases on credit or access short-term loans. Credit cards are widely used for both personal and business purposes, and they offer convenience and flexibility by allowing customers to make payments over time. Banks benefit from the interest charged on unpaid credit card balances, while customers enjoy rewards and benefits tied to card usage.

6. Foreign Exchange:

Commercial banks play a pivotal role in facilitating foreign exchange transactions. They help individuals and businesses convert one currency into another, a service that is essential for international trade and travel. In addition to currency conversion, banks offer remittance services, enabling customers to send money across borders efficiently. This function is particularly important in a globalized economy where cross-border transactions are commonplace.

7. Trust Services:

Commercial banks also offer trust and estate planning services. These services help individuals and businesses manage their wealth, ensuring that assets are preserved and transferred to beneficiaries in an organized manner. Trust services include estate administration, trust management, and acting as trustees to safeguard assets on behalf of clients. These offerings are especially valuable for customers looking to plan for the future and manage their financial legacies.

8. Investment Services:

In addition to traditional banking services, commercial banks provide basic investment services. They offer products such as savings accounts, certificates of deposit (CDs), money market accounts, and mutual funds. While commercial banks typically do not engage in high-level investment activities like investment banks, they provide customers with safe and accessible investment options to grow their savings over time. These products are suitable for customers looking for conservative investment strategies with minimal risk.

In conclusion, commercial banks provide a wide range of financial services to individuals and businesses and play a critical role in the economy by accepting deposits, providing loans, and facilitating the transfer of funds.

L. DIFFERENCE BETWEEN CENTRAL BANK AND COMMERCIAL BANK

About	Central bank	Commercial banks
Purpose	Central banks are created and empowered by the government to serve as the central monetary authority of a country	commercial banks are profit-oriented financial institutions that provide financial services to individuals and businesses.
Ownership	Central banks are owned by the government	commercial banks are owned by private individuals, corporations, or a combination of both.
Role in the economy	Central banks play a key role in maintaining the stability of the financial system, controlling inflation, and	commercial banks play a critical role in facilitating the flow of credit and promoting economic

	implementing monetary policy.	growth.
Powers	Central banks have the power to issue currency, regulate the money supply, and control interest rates	commercial banks do not have these powers.
Regulation	Central banks are usually responsible for regulating and supervising the activities of commercial banks	commercial banks are regulated by the central bank and other financial regulators.
Profitability	Central banks do not have a profit motive, as their goal is to maintain financial stability and support economic growth.	commercial banks are profit-oriented and aim to generate income through their lending and investment activities.

Exhibit1.10: Differece between Cental Banks and Commercial Banks

In conclusion, while both central banks and commercial banks play important roles in the economy, they have distinct purposes, powers, and responsibilities, and serve different segments of the financial system.

CHAPTER SUMMARY

CENTRAL BANK

In conclusion, while both central banks and commercial banks play important roles in the economy, they have distinct purposes, powers, and responsibilities, and serve different segments of the financial system.

The chapter on Central Bank provides a thorough understanding of the central banking system, particularly in the context of India, with a special emphasis on the Reserve Bank of India (RBI). The chapter begins by introducing the concept of the Central Bank, highlighting its pivotal role in overseeing a country's monetary system, managing interest rates, issuing currency, and acting as a regulator and supervisor of the financial system.

The core functions of the Central Bank are explained in detail, emphasizing its responsibilities in controlling inflation, managing foreign reserves, and ensuring financial stability. The discussion then shifts to the RBI, exploring its traditional functions, such as currency issuance and foreign exchange management, alongside its developmental and supervisory functions. The chapter outlines how the RBI has played a crucial role in fostering economic growth and financial inclusion in India through various policies and initiatives aimed at rural development and expanding access to financial services.

The objectives of the RBI are to ensure price stability, promote economic growth, and maintain financial system stability, illustrating the central bank's dual mandate of controlling inflation while fostering economic development.

Furthermore, the chapter distinguishes between Central Banks and Commercial Banks. While the RBI, as a central bank, focuses on broader economic stability and regulatory oversight, commercial banks serve the public by accepting deposits, providing loans, and offering financial services. The chapter emphasizes the importance of commercial banks in India's financial ecosystem, particularly their role in mobilizing savings and providing credit for personal and business growth.

The conclusion of this chapter highlights the importance of both central and commercial banks in driving economic development, with the Central Bank (RBI) playing a strategic regulatory role, and commercial banks supporting day-to-day economic activities through financial services. The distinction between the two types of banks is crucial in understanding their unique yet complementary roles in the financial system.

CASE STUDIES

Case Study 1.1: The Role of RBI in Managing the 2008 Financial Crisis

During the Global Financial Crisis (2008-2009), the Reserve Bank of India (RBI) played a crucial role in safeguarding the Indian economy from severe disruption. Although India was not as deeply affected as Western economies, the crisis created significant challenges, particularly in terms of liquidity shortages, falling demand for exports, and slowing economic growth. The sudden tightening of global credit markets posed a serious threat to India's banking system and broader financial sector. In response, the RBI took decisive actions to mitigate the impact of the crisis on the Indian economy.

One of the first measures was the liquidity infusion into the banking system. The RBI reduced the Cash Reserve Ratio (CRR), Statutory Liquidity Ratio (SLR), and the repo rate to encourage banks to lend more freely and maintain the flow of credit to businesses and consumers. These reductions allowed banks to release more funds, helping businesses sustain operations despite the global credit squeeze. Additionally, the RBI implemented Special Market Operations (SMO), which involved buying government securities and foreign exchange swaps to stabilize the rupee and provide liquidity in the financial markets. These measures helped prevent excessive volatility in the exchange rate and ensured the stability of India's financial markets.

In cooperation with commercial banks, the RBI stressed the importance of sound lending practices and risk management to avoid a surge in non-performing assets (NPAs) during the crisis. By working closely with banks, the RBI ensured that lending remained prudent, while still making credit available to sectors in need. As part of its supervisory functions, the RBI also strengthened regulatory oversight, requiring banks to maintain adequate capital buffers to absorb potential losses. These steps helped preserve financial stability during the global downturn, allowing India to emerge from the crisis with minimal damage compared to many other countries.

Questions Based on the Case:

i. How did the RBI's reduction of the Cash Reserve Ratio (CRR) and Statutory Liquidity Ratio (SLR) help the Indian banking system during the 2008 financial crisis?

ii. What was the significance of the RBI's Special Market Operations (SMO) during the financial crisis, and how did these operations stabilize the economy?

iii. In what ways did the RBI's cooperation with commercial banks and its focus on regulatory oversight help mitigate the risks associated with the global financial crisis in India?

Case Study 1.2: RBI's Role in Demonetization (2016)

In November 2016, the Indian government, in collaboration with the Reserve Bank of India (RBI), initiated one of the most significant monetary reforms in the country's history—demonetization. The government demonetized ₹500 and ₹1,000 notes, rendering them invalid as legal tender, which affected nearly 86% of the currency in circulation. The move was aimed at curbing black money, counterfeit currency, and corruption. The RBI, as the central bank of the country, played a pivotal role in executing and managing this sudden change in the monetary landscape.

During demonetization, the RBI's role was multifaceted. It had the responsibility of printing new ₹500 and ₹2,000 notes, ensuring their smooth distribution across the country. Managing liquidity during this period was a significant challenge as banks faced huge demand for cash. To mitigate this, the RBI introduced several liquidity management measures, such as increasing the supply of smaller denomination notes and facilitating cash withdrawal limits to prevent hoarding and ensure equitable distribution of new currency.

Another critical function of the RBI during demonetization was maintaining public confidence in the banking system. As people queued up to exchange old currency notes, banks experienced unprecedented footfalls. The RBI had to work closely with commercial banks to ensure smooth functioning and adequate availability of cash. It also monitored the currency flow through its supervisory framework, ensuring that banks complied with the guidelines and regulations related to the exchange process.

Additionally, the RBI's role in demonetization highlighted its developmental functions. Through initiatives like encouraging digital transactions, the central bank supported the transition to a less-cash economy, promoting long-term financial inclusion and digitization of payments. Demonetization had far-reaching economic implications, but the RBI's effective management of currency and liquidity helped stabilize the situation and restore normalcy in a relatively short period.

Questions Based on the Case:

i.   What were the primary challenges faced by the RBI during the demonetization process in 2016, and how did it address the issue of liquidity management?

ii. How did the RBI's supervisory role help maintain public confidence and smooth functioning of banks during the demonetization period?

iii. In what ways did the RBI promote digital transactions and financial inclusion as part of its developmental functions during and after demonetization?

Case Study 1.3: The RBI's Supervisory Role in the Yes Bank Crisis (2020)

In 2020, the Reserve Bank of India (RBI) played a crucial role in managing the Yes Bank crisis, which posed a significant threat to

India's banking sector. Yes Bank, one of the largest private sector banks in India, faced a liquidity crisis due to its rising non-performing assets (NPAs) and exposure to risky loans. The bank's financial health deteriorated, causing a sharp decline in its stock price and prompting a loss of confidence among depositors. To prevent a wider financial contagion, the RBI intervened with timely regulatory measures.

The RBI's supervisory function was instrumental in addressing the crisis. Initially, it imposed a moratorium on Yes Bank, restricting the withdrawal limit for depositors to ₹50,000. This move was designed to prevent a bank run and ensure stability in the broader banking system. Simultaneously, the RBI worked to create a restructuring plan, under which the State Bank of India (SBI) and other investors injected capital to revive the bank. The RBI's coordination with government agencies, other commercial banks, and market participants was essential in stabilizing Yes Bank.

Moreover, the crisis underscored the RBI's role in strengthening regulatory oversight in the banking sector. It took steps to monitor the health of other banks more closely, ensuring that they adhered to prudent lending practices and maintained adequate capital reserves. This case highlighted the need for improved risk management practices across the banking industry, particularly in terms of identifying and mitigating credit risk.

The Yes Bank crisis also shed light on the RBI's developmental and supervisory functions. By ensuring the restructuring of Yes Bank, the RBI helped restore confidence in the private banking sector and safeguarded the interests of depositors and investors. The RBI's swift action in handling the crisis demonstrated its commitment to financial stability and its role as a guardian of the Indian banking system.

Questions Based on the Case:

i. What were the key measures taken by the RBI to prevent the collapse of Yes Bank, and how did these actions help restore stability in the banking sector?

ii. How did the RBI's supervisory function evolve after the Yes Bank crisis, particularly in terms of regulatory oversight and risk management?

iii. What lessons can be learned from the Yes Bank crisis regarding the importance of capital reserves and prudent lending practices in the Indian banking system?

Case Study 1.4: The RBI's Role in Handling the IL&FS Crisis (2018)

In 2018, India faced a significant financial crisis when Infrastructure Leasing & Financial Services (IL&FS), a major infrastructure financing and development company, defaulted on its debt obligations. With over ₹91,000 crore in debt, IL&FS's default triggered fears of a broader financial contagion, particularly affecting India's non-banking financial companies (NBFCs) and the financial sector. The Reserve Bank of India (RBI) played a critical role in managing the aftermath of this crisis, focusing on maintaining financial stability and ensuring that the systemic risk did not spread across the broader economy.

The crisis unfolded when IL&FS, a key player in infrastructure finance, failed to meet its repayment obligations, leading to a liquidity crunch in the market. This raised concerns about the solvency of NBFCs, as they were heavily dependent on short-term borrowing to finance long-term infrastructure projects. The RBI immediately stepped in with several measures to stabilize the situation. Its supervisory function became critical as it closely monitored NBFCs and other financial institutions for any signs of distress.

One of the RBI's primary responses was to inject liquidity into the system to prevent a credit crunch. It undertook open market operations (OMOs) to purchase government securities, thus releasing liquidity into the banking system. Additionally, the RBI temporarily eased certain regulatory norms, allowing banks and NBFCs to manage their liquidity positions more effectively. By doing so, the RBI ensured that NBFCs and banks could continue to lend and meet their obligations, thus preventing a complete freeze in the financial markets.

In terms of its developmental functions, the RBI also worked on improving the regulatory framework for NBFCs. The crisis had exposed weaknesses in the sector, particularly in terms of risk management and corporate governance. As a result, the RBI tightened norms around asset-liability management and capital adequacy for NBFCs, aiming to reduce systemic risks in the future. It also improved its supervisory oversight by conducting more rigorous inspections and stress tests of NBFCs to ensure their financial health.

This case underscored the RBI's crucial role as the central authority responsible for ensuring the stability of the financial system. By effectively managing the liquidity crunch and tightening regulations for NBFCs, the RBI mitigated the potential fallout of the IL&FS crisis and restored confidence in India's financial markets.

Questions Based on the Case:

i. How did the RBI's liquidity management measures, such as open market operations, help mitigate the impact of the IL&FS crisis on the Indian financial system?

ii. What were the key weaknesses in the NBFC sector that the IL&FS crisis exposed, and how did the RBI address these issues through regulatory changes?

iii. How did the RBI's supervisory function evolve in response to the IL&FS crisis, particularly in its approach to monitoring and managing systemic risks in the financial sector?

MONETARY POLICY

Learning Objectives:

- *Understand what monetary policy is and why it is important for managing money and the economy in India.*
- *Learn the main goals of monetary policy, like controlling inflation, supporting economic growth, and keeping the financial system stable.*
- *Explore the tools the Reserve Bank of India (RBI) uses to achieve these goals, such as interest rates and money supply controls.*
- *Understand the different types of monetary policies, like policies that help the economy grow and those that slow it down when needed.*
- *Learn about the role of the Monetary Policy Committee in setting and managing these policies in India.*

Prof. A. Narasimha Rao

K T S S Satyanarayana

MONETARY POLICY

"...the primary objective of monetary policy is to maintain price stability while keeping in mind the objective of growth."

-Preamble to the RBI Act1934

Monetary policy refers to the actions taken by a central bank, to control the money supply and interest rates in an economy. The primary tools of monetary policy are setting interest rates and adjusting the money supply through the buying and selling of government securities. The goal of monetary policy is to stabilize the economy by controlling inflation and promoting economic growth.

Money supply

The money supply refers to the total amount of money available in an economy at any given time. It includes not only the currency in circulation but also the money held in checking and savings accounts at financial institutions. Central banks, such as the Federal Reserve in the United States, play a key role in controlling the money supply through various tools like open market operations and setting reserve requirements for banks. The primary goal of managing the money supply is to stabilize the economy by controlling inflation and promoting economic growth.

Inflation

Inflation is the rate at which the general level of prices for goods and services is rising, and subsequently, purchasing power is falling. Central banks, such as the Federal Reserve in the United States, use monetary policy to target a specific rate of inflation. Inflation can have negative effects on an economy, such as reducing purchasing power for consumers and increasing uncertainty for businesses. However, a moderate rate of inflation can also indicate a healthy economy.

Economic growth:

Economic growth refers to the increase in the value of goods and services produced by an economy over a period of time. It is usually measured as the percentage change in gross domestic product (GDP) over a period of time, typically a year. Economic growth is an important indicator of a country's economic health and well-being, as it is associated with an increase in the standard of living and employment opportunities. Economic growth can be driven by a variety of factors, including increased productivity, population growth, and government policies that promote investment and trade.

A. Monetary Policy in India

The Reserve Bank of India (RBI) is the central bank of India and is responsible for implementing monetary policy in the country. The RBI uses a variety of tools to control the money supply and interest rates, including setting reserve requirements for banks, open market operations, and changing the policy interest rate. The main objectives of monetary policy in India are to maintain price stability, support economic growth, and ensure financial stability.

The RBI's primary tool for achieving its objectives is the policy repo rate, which is the rate at which it lends money to commercial banks. By changing the policy repo rate, the RBI can influence the overall interest rate environment in the economy, which in turn can affect investment, consumption, and inflation. The RBI also uses other tools like cash reserve ratio, statutory liquidity ratio and open market operations to control money supply in the economy.

In recent years, the RBI has focused on maintaining low inflation while supporting economic growth. In order to achieve this, the RBI has used a combination of monetary policy tools and communication strategies to provide guidance to market participants and anchor inflation expectations.

B. Objectives of Monetary Policy in India

Monetary policy in India is crafted by the Reserve Bank of India (RBI) with the aim of achieving several key objectives that contribute to the overall economic stability and growth of the country.

Below are the primary goals of the RBI's monetary policy:

1. Price Stability:

One of the foremost objectives of the RBI's monetary policy is to maintain price stability, which essentially means keeping inflation within a controlled and acceptable range. This helps to ensure that prices of goods and services do not rise too rapidly, protecting the purchasing power of consumers and maintaining economic stability. Price stability is critical as uncontrolled inflation can lead to higher costs of living, reduced savings, and a decrease in consumer confidence. The RBI sets an inflation target and adjusts interest rates or undertakes other measures to keep inflation within that target, currently set by the Government of India.

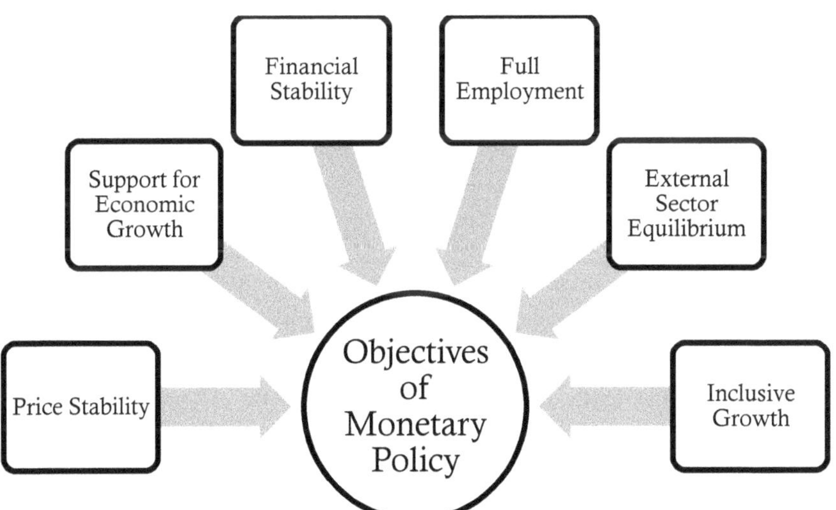

Exhibit2.1: Objectives of Monetary Policy

2. Support for Economic Growth:

Monetary policy in India also plays a pivotal role in fostering economic growth. By ensuring a balanced money supply and favorable interest rates, the RBI promotes investment by businesses and consumption by individuals, both of which are essential drivers of economic growth. Lower interest rates, for instance, reduce the cost of borrowing, making it easier for companies to invest in new projects, thereby boosting employment and overall economic activity. The RBI seeks to strike a balance between curbing inflation and providing enough liquidity to support growth.

3. Financial Stability:

Ensuring the stability of the financial system is another critical goal of the RBI. This includes promoting the smooth functioning of financial markets, ensuring the health of financial institutions, and mitigating systemic risks that could lead to crises. The RBI monitors various financial indicators and implements policies to prevent excessive volatility or instability in financial markets, which could otherwise disrupt economic activity and lead to a loss of confidence among investors and consumers alike.

4. Full Employment:

The RBI also works toward the goal of full employment, aiming to maximize job opportunities across the economy. Monetary policies that promote investment and economic growth contribute to creating more jobs, thereby reducing unemployment levels. While full employment is an ambitious target, the RBI's efforts to maintain stable inflation, foster economic growth, and ensure financial stability collectively support the achievement of this goal.

5. External Sector Equilibrium:

Another objective of the RBI's monetary policy is to maintain equilibrium in the external sector, which involves managing the exchange rate and ensuring balance in foreign trade. Stability in the external sector is crucial to maintaining investor confidence and ensuring that India's exports remain competitive in global markets. The RBI takes measures to stabilize the exchange rate and ensure that external imbalances do not negatively affect domestic economic conditions.

6. Inclusive Growth:

Inclusive growth is a key priority for the RBI, which aims to ensure that the benefits of economic expansion reach all sections of society, particularly the weaker and marginalized groups. This involves making financial services more accessible and encouraging credit flow to sectors such as agriculture, small and medium enterprises, and rural areas. The RBI uses targeted policies to support inclusive financial development, thereby ensuring that growth is equitable and reduces income disparities.

To achieve these objectives, the RBI uses a variety of monetary policy tools, such as setting interest rates, manipulating the money supply, and providing liquidity to the banking system.

C. RBI tools to achieve the Objectives of Monetary Policy

The Reserve Bank of India (RBI) uses a variety of tools to achieve the objectives of monetary policy, which include:

1. Repo rate:

The repo rate is one of the most important tools the Reserve Bank of India (RBI) uses to achieve its monetary policy objectives. Essentially, it's the interest rate at which the RBI lends money to commercial banks when they face short-term liquidity needs. Imagine a bank that needs funds overnight to meet its obligations, so it borrows from the RBI by offering government securities with the agreement to buy them back later. This is what happens under a repo transaction.

Now, the RBI adjusts the repo rate to control the economy, specifically to manage inflation and stimulate growth. For example, when inflation starts rising—say prices of essential goods are increasing too quickly—the RBI might raise the repo rate. This makes it more expensive for banks to borrow money from the RBI, so they, in turn, raise the interest rates for their customers. Businesses and consumers now find it more costly to take loans, reducing their spending. As demand decreases, inflation slows down. In this way, a higher repo rate helps to keep inflation in check.

On the flip side, if the economy is slowing down, with businesses struggling and unemployment rising, the RBI might lower the repo rate. This makes borrowing cheaper for banks, and in turn, banks lower interest rates for consumers and businesses. With loans now more affordable, people and companies are encouraged to borrow, spend, and invest, stimulating economic activity. Thus, a lower repo rate helps revitalize the economy during sluggish times.

Tools to Achive - Objectives of Monetary Policy	Repo Rate
	Reverse Repo Rate
	Cash Reserve Ratio
	Statutory Liquidity Ratio
	Open Market Operations
	Margin Standing Facility
	Bank Rate
	Liquidity Adjustment Facility
	Market Stabilisation Rate

Exhibit 2.2: Monetary Policy Tools

2. Reverse repo rate:

The reverse repo rate is another critical tool that the Reserve Bank of India (RBI) uses to manage liquidity in the economy. In simple terms, it's the interest rate at which the RBI borrows money from commercial banks. This tool comes into play when the RBI wants to manage excess liquidity in the banking system.

Imagine a scenario where there's too much money circulating in the economy, leading to inflationary pressures—prices of goods are rising because people and businesses have excess funds to spend. To tackle this, the RBI uses the reverse repo rate to encourage banks to park their surplus funds with the central bank instead of lending them out to the public. When the RBI increases the reverse repo rate, it makes it more attractive for banks to lend money to the RBI, as they earn a higher interest on these deposits. This, in turn, reduces the amount of money available for lending in the market, helping to bring down inflation.

For example, if a bank has excess funds and the reverse repo rate is attractive, it will prefer to lend that money to the RBI instead of making riskier loans to businesses or individuals. This helps absorb the extra liquidity in the system and keeps inflation in check. Conversely, if the RBI wants to encourage lending and stimulate economic activity, it might lower the reverse repo rate, making it less appealing for banks to park their money with the RBI. This encourages banks to lend more, boosting economic activity through increased investments and consumption.

In this way, the reverse repo rate serves as a balancing mechanism, ensuring that there's neither too much nor too little liquidity in the economy, helping maintain financial stability.

3. Cash Reserve Ratio (CRR) and Statutory Liquidity Ratio (SLR):

The Cash Reserve Ratio (CRR) and Statutory Liquidity Ratio (SLR) are two key tools that the Reserve Bank of India (RBI) uses to control liquidity and ensure stability in the banking system. Both of these are regulatory requirements that commercial banks must adhere to, and they play a vital role in shaping monetary policy and financial stability in the country.

CRR refers to the percentage of a bank's total deposits that must be kept as reserves with the RBI. This amount cannot be used for lending or investment purposes by the bank. The primary objective of CRR is to ensure that banks always have a portion of their deposits in safe custody with the central bank, which helps control liquidity in the economy. When the RBI wants to reduce the money supply to combat inflation, it increases the CRR. This reduces the funds available to banks for lending and investment, thereby tightening liquidity in the market. For instance, if a bank receives deposits of ₹100 crore and the CRR is set at 4%, the bank must keep ₹4 crore with the RBI and can only use the remaining ₹96 crore for lending or other activities.

On the other hand, when the RBI lowers the CRR, banks have more funds at their disposal for lending, which can stimulate economic activity by encouraging investments and consumption. This tool becomes especially important when the economy needs a boost or during times of low inflation.

SLR is another regulatory requirement, but instead of keeping reserves with the RBI, banks are required to hold a certain percentage of their deposits in the form of liquid assets, such as government bonds, gold, or cash. This percentage is known as the Statutory Liquidity Ratio. SLR ensures that banks maintain a cushion of liquid assets that can be easily converted into cash to meet their financial obligations. It also serves as a way for the RBI to control credit growth and manage inflation.

When the RBI increases the SLR, banks are required to hold more of their deposits in safe, liquid assets, which reduces the amount of money available for lending. This can help cool down an overheating economy by reducing the supply of credit. Conversely, lowering the SLR frees up more funds for banks to lend, which can stimulate economic growth, especially during periods of sluggish economic activity.

Both CRR and SLR are essential tools in maintaining financial discipline and ensuring that banks remain solvent while playing a crucial role in regulating the overall money supply in the economy. By adjusting these ratios, the RBI can influence the availability of credit, manage inflation, and ensure the smooth functioning of the banking sector.

4. Open market operations:

Open market operations (OMOs) are a critical tool used by the Reserve Bank of India (RBI) to regulate the money supply and influence interest rates in the economy. OMOs involve the buying and selling of government securities in the open market. This mechanism allows the central bank to adjust the liquidity available in the banking system, directly impacting economic activity.

When the RBI wants to increase the money supply, it purchases government securities from banks and financial institutions. This influx of funds into the banking system enhances the liquidity available to banks, allowing them to lend more to businesses and consumers. For example, if the RBI buys ₹1,000 crore worth of government bonds from commercial banks, those banks receive cash in exchange, which they can then use to extend loans to customers. This increase in lending can stimulate economic growth by encouraging investments and spending, ultimately leading to higher demand for goods and services.

5. Marginal Standing Facility (MSF):

The Marginal Standing Facility (MSF) is a crucial tool used by the Reserve Bank of India (RBI) to provide liquidity support to banks in times of need. It allows banks to borrow funds overnight from the RBI at a higher interest rate than the repo rate, thereby acting as a safety net for financial institutions facing short-term liquidity shortages.

When banks experience unexpected cash flow issues, they can utilize the MSF to access funds quickly. For instance, if a bank is short on liquidity at the end of the day due to unexpected withdrawals or loan demands, it can borrow from the RBI at the MSF rate, which is typically set above the repo rate. This facility ensures that banks can meet their immediate financial obligations without disrupting their operations or the overall stability of the banking system.

The MSF not only provides a reliable source of funds but also helps in stabilizing the financial system by ensuring that banks remain solvent and can continue to lend to businesses and consumers. By maintaining this safety net, the RBI fosters confidence in the banking sector, encouraging banks to manage their liquidity effectively while also supporting economic growth during challenging times.

6. Bank Rate:

The bank rate is another significant tool employed by the Reserve Bank of India (RBI) to influence monetary policy and manage the economy. It refers to the rate at which the central bank lends money to commercial banks, typically for long-term loans. By adjusting the bank rate, the RBI can impact the cost of borrowing for banks, which subsequently affects interest rates for consumers and businesses.

When the RBI raises the bank rate, borrowing becomes more expensive for commercial banks. This often leads to higher interest rates for loans and credit, which can dampen consumer spending and investment, thereby helping to control inflation. For example, if the RBI increases the bank rate to combat rising prices, banks will likely raise their lending rates, making it costlier for individuals and businesses to take out loans. This reduction in borrowing can help cool down an overheating economy.

Conversely, when the RBI lowers the bank rate, it encourages banks to borrow more at a lower cost, leading to decreased interest rates for loans. This stimulates borrowing and investment, fostering economic growth. For instance, a lower bank rate might incentivize a business to expand operations by taking a loan, thereby creating jobs and driving economic activity. Thus, the bank rate serves as a vital mechanism for the RBI to navigate the delicate balance between controlling inflation and supporting economic growth.

7. Liquidity adjustment facility (LAF):

The Liquidity Adjustment Facility (LAF) is a crucial tool used by the Reserve Bank of India (RBI) to manage liquidity in the banking system and influence short-term interest rates. It allows banks to borrow money through repurchase agreements (repos) or lend money to the central bank through reverse repos, effectively regulating the money supply in the economy.

When banks face short-term liquidity shortages, they can use the LAF to borrow funds from the RBI. For instance, if a bank experiences unexpected withdrawals and needs immediate cash to meet its obligations, it can opt for a repo under the LAF. In this scenario, the bank agrees to sell securities to the RBI with a commitment to repurchase them at a later date, typically at a slightly higher price, which reflects the interest rate. This borrowing option ensures that banks can maintain stability without resorting to drastic measures, thus supporting the overall financial system.

On the flip side, when the RBI wants to absorb excess liquidity from the market—perhaps to curb inflation—it can utilize reverse repos under the LAF. In this case, banks lend their excess funds to the RBI, receiving securities in return. For example, if banks are flush with cash due to a surge in deposits but the economy shows signs of overheating, the RBI might increase the reverse repo rate, encouraging banks to park their surplus funds with the central bank instead of lending them out. This dual mechanism of borrowing and lending through the LAF allows the RBI to fine-tune liquidity conditions, helping to maintain economic stability and control inflation effectively.

8. Market Stabilization Scheme (MSS):

The Market Stabilization Scheme (MSS) is a monetary policy tool employed by the Reserve Bank of India (RBI) to manage excess liquidity in the financial system and stabilize the market. Under this scheme, the RBI issues government securities to absorb surplus liquidity when it is concerned about inflationary pressures or an overheated economy.

For example, if there is a sudden influx of funds into the banking system due to seasonal factors, like the harvest season, banks may find themselves with more cash than they can lend. This excess liquidity can lead to lower interest rates and potentially fuel inflation. In response, the RBI may initiate the MSS by issuing treasury bills or bonds, effectively absorbing the excess cash from the market. By selling these securities, the RBI draws money out of circulation, which helps to tighten liquidity conditions and maintain price stability.

Conversely, the MSS can also be used to inject liquidity when the economy is sluggish. If the RBI wants to encourage spending and investment, it can purchase government securities back from the market, thereby infusing cash into the financial system. For instance, during an economic slowdown, this action can lower interest rates, making borrowing cheaper and stimulating economic activity. Through the Market Stabilization Scheme, the RBI can effectively manage liquidity in a flexible manner, ensuring that the financial system remains stable while aligning with broader economic goals.

All these tools are used to control the money supply and interest rates in the economy to achieve the objectives of monetary policy, like price stability, support for economic growth, financial stability, and full employment.

D. ROLE OF MONETARY POLICY IN INDIA

Monetary policy plays a crucial role in shaping the Indian economy by directly influencing the overall level of interest rates and the money supply. The Reserve Bank of India (RBI) is the central authority responsible for implementing these policies, utilizing a range of tools to achieve its primary objectives. One of the foremost goals is to maintain price stability, which involves keeping inflation within a targeted range. By controlling inflation, the RBI ensures that the purchasing power of the Indian currency remains stable, providing a conducive environment for economic activities.

Supporting economic growth is another vital objective of monetary policy. The RBI promotes investment and consumption by adjusting interest rates, making borrowing cheaper during times of economic slowdown. For instance, lowering the repo rate can encourage banks to reduce their lending rates, stimulating consumer spending and business investments. This proactive approach is essential for fostering sustainable economic growth, particularly in a rapidly developing economy like India.

Financial stability is also a significant focus of the RBI's monetary policy. By monitoring and regulating the banking sector, the RBI ensures the smooth functioning of financial markets and institutions. This oversight helps prevent systemic risks that could arise from excessive lending or market volatility, ultimately safeguarding the overall health of the financial system.

Additionally, the RBI aims for full employment, which means maximizing the number of people employed in the economy. By adjusting monetary policy to encourage economic activity, the central bank can help create jobs and reduce unemployment rates. This focus on employment is critical, especially in a country with a large workforce.

The RBI also recognizes the importance of the external sector, working to maintain equilibrium in foreign exchange markets. This involves ensuring stability in the exchange rate, which is vital for promoting exports and managing trade balances. A stable currency can bolster investor confidence and support international trade, further contributing to economic growth.

Lastly, inclusive growth is a core principle of the RBI's monetary policy. The central bank strives to ensure that the benefits of economic development reach all sections of society, particularly marginalized groups. By promoting financial inclusion and access to credit, the RBI aims to empower these communities, enabling them to participate actively in the economy.

In summary, monetary policy in India serves as a critical lever for the RBI to influence economic conditions. Through careful management of interest rates and the money supply, the RBI works to maintain price stability, support economic growth, ensure financial stability, achieve full employment, and promote inclusive growth, ultimately shaping a resilient and thriving economy.

Some of the key roles of monetary policy in India include:

1. Inflation control:

Monetary policy in India serves several critical roles, with one of the most significant being inflation control. Inflation refers to the rate at which the general level of prices for goods and services rises, leading to a decrease in purchasing power. The Reserve Bank of India (RBI) aims to maintain price stability, which is vital for economic health. By controlling inflation, the RBI ensures that the currency retains its value, fostering confidence among consumers and investors.

To achieve this, the RBI employs various tools, such as adjusting the repo rate. For example, if inflation is rising above the target range, the RBI may increase the repo rate. This action makes borrowing more expensive for banks, which, in turn, raises interest rates for consumers and businesses. As a result, higher interest rates can lead to reduced spending and investment, cooling off demand in the economy and helping to bring inflation down.

Additionally, the RBI monitors various economic indicators, including the Consumer Price Index (CPI), which measures changes in the price level of a basket of consumer goods and services. If the CPI shows a significant increase, indicating rising inflation, the RBI may take preemptive measures to stabilize prices. For instance, if inflation trends are concerning, the RBI might implement open market operations to sell government securities, effectively reducing the money supply in circulation. This reduction can help ease inflationary pressures by curbing excess liquidity in the economy.

Overall, by actively managing inflation through monetary policy, the RBI plays a vital role in ensuring economic stability and fostering sustainable growth in India.

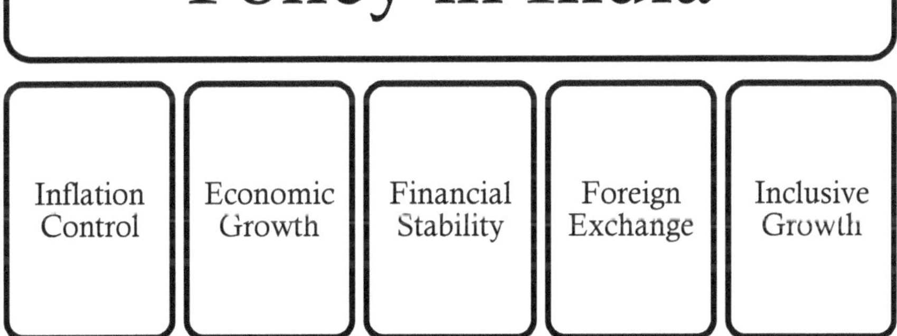

Exhibit 2.3: Role of Monetary Policy in India

2. Economic growth:

Monetary policy in India also plays a key role in promoting economic growth. Economic growth refers to an increase in the production of goods and services in the economy over time, leading to higher income levels and improved standards of living. The

Reserve Bank of India (RBI) supports growth by managing the availability and cost of money through its monetary tools.

One way the RBI promotes growth is by adjusting interest rates, particularly the repo rate. For example, if the economy is slowing down and needs a boost, the RBI may lower the repo rate. A lower repo rate means that borrowing costs for banks decrease, which allows them to lend money to businesses and consumers at lower interest rates. As a result, businesses are more likely to invest in expansion, and consumers are more inclined to borrow for big purchases like homes or cars. This increased spending and investment fuel economic activity, leading to job creation and higher production levels, thereby stimulating growth.

The RBI also uses liquidity management tools like the Cash Reserve Ratio (CRR) and Statutory Liquidity Ratio (SLR) to ensure there's enough money circulating in the economy. For instance, during periods of sluggish growth, the RBI may reduce the CRR, allowing banks to lend more money. This increased liquidity enables businesses to access funds for investment, further supporting economic growth.

Moreover, through initiatives like the Priority Sector Lending (PSL) framework, the RBI ensures that sectors critical to economic development, such as agriculture, small industries, and housing, receive adequate financing. By guiding funds to these key sectors, the RBI helps stimulate economic growth that benefits a wide range of industries and population groups.

Thus, by carefully adjusting monetary policy to create a conducive environment for investment and consumption, the RBI plays a pivotal role in fostering long-term economic growth in India.

3. Financial stability:

Monetary policy in India also plays a vital role in ensuring financial stability, which involves maintaining a sound and resilient financial system that can withstand shocks and continue to function smoothly.

The Reserve Bank of India (RBI) takes several measures through its monetary tools to safeguard the stability of financial institutions, markets, and the overall banking system.

One of the key ways the RBI promotes financial stability is by regulating interest rates and managing liquidity. For instance, if there is excess liquidity in the financial system, it can lead to overheating of the economy, potentially causing asset bubbles, where the prices of assets like real estate or stocks rise rapidly and unsustainably. To prevent this, the RBI might increase the Cash Reserve Ratio (CRR) or the Statutory Liquidity Ratio (SLR), requiring banks to hold more funds as reserves. This reduces the amount of money banks have available to lend, cooling down excessive borrowing and speculation, thus protecting the financial system from instability.

The RBI also conducts regular supervision of banks and financial institutions. For example, through periodic inspections and stress tests, the central bank evaluates the health of banks, ensuring that they are managing risks effectively and maintaining adequate capital reserves. In cases where a bank is facing financial difficulties, the RBI can intervene by providing liquidity support through the Marginal Standing Facility (MSF) or other emergency measures, preventing the bank's troubles from spreading to the broader financial system.

Another critical tool is the regulation of Non-Banking Financial Companies (NBFCs). The RBI monitors these institutions to ensure they follow prudential guidelines, as NBFCs play a significant role in providing credit to underserved sectors. By keeping a check on their operations, the RBI helps avoid risks that could spill over into the banking sector or disrupt financial markets.

Through measures like these, the RBI's monetary policy ensures that the financial system remains robust, capable of withstanding economic shocks, and resilient enough to support the broader economy without facing crises. Financial stability, therefore, is crucial for maintaining public confidence in the banking system and fostering sustainable economic growth.

4. Foreign exchange:

Monetary policy in India also plays a significant role in managing foreign exchange and ensuring stability in the external sector. The Reserve Bank of India (RBI) uses various tools to influence the exchange rate of the Indian rupee and maintain a balance between imports and exports, thereby promoting external sector stability.

One way the RBI manages foreign exchange is through interventions in the foreign exchange market. For instance, if the Indian rupee depreciates significantly against major foreign currencies, making imports more expensive and leading to inflationary pressures, the RBI might step in and sell foreign currency reserves to prop up the value of the rupee. This helps prevent a sharp decline in the rupee's value, stabilizing exchange rates. Conversely, if the rupee appreciates too much, making Indian exports less competitive in international markets, the RBI might buy foreign currency to prevent the rupee from strengthening excessively.

Open Market Operations (OMOs) are also used to influence foreign exchange indirectly. By adjusting domestic liquidity, the RBI can affect interest rates, which in turn influence capital flows. For example, if the RBI lowers interest rates to stimulate the economy, it may lead to an outflow of foreign investments as investors seek better returns elsewhere, affecting the rupee's exchange rate. To prevent volatility in such scenarios, the RBI carefully manages these flows.

The RBI also uses foreign exchange reserves as a buffer to handle external shocks. For instance, during global economic crises or periods of geopolitical uncertainty, countries may experience sudden capital outflows or disruptions in trade. In such cases, the RBI can use its reserves to ensure that there is enough foreign currency available for essential imports, like oil, and to manage exchange rate fluctuations.

Moreover, the RBI keeps an eye on the current account deficit, which reflects the difference between a country's imports and exports. If the deficit widens too much, indicating that the country is importing significantly more than it exports, the RBI might adjust its monetary policy to promote exports by keeping interest rates low or encouraging investment in export-oriented industries.

By managing foreign exchange effectively, the RBI helps maintain a stable and predictable environment for international trade and investment. This stability not only protects the domestic economy from external shocks but also ensures that India remains competitive in the global market.

5. Inclusive growth:

Monetary policy in India also plays a crucial role in promoting inclusive growth, ensuring that the benefits of economic development reach all sections of society, particularly the marginalized and economically weaker sections. The Reserve Bank of India (RBI), through its various tools and strategies, aims to create an environment where growth is not only robust but also equitable.

One of the key ways the RBI promotes inclusive growth is by ensuring access to affordable credit, especially for sectors that are critical to employment generation, such as agriculture, small and medium enterprises (SMEs), and microfinance. For instance, the RBI sets priority sector lending targets for commercial banks, mandating that a certain percentage of their lending must go to sectors like agriculture, education, and affordable housing. This ensures that credit reaches those areas of the economy that are often underserved by traditional banking systems, allowing small farmers and entrepreneurs to access the funds they need to grow their businesses and improve their livelihoods.

Additionally, the RBI plays a significant role in financial inclusion by encouraging banks to open branches in rural and semi-urban areas. This is achieved through policy measures that make it easier for banks to expand into these regions, where a significant portion of the population still lacks access to formal banking services. By promoting the spread of banking infrastructure and digital payment systems, the RBI helps bring more people into the formal financial fold, allowing them to save, invest, and borrow more efficiently.

Another important aspect of inclusive growth is inflation control. High inflation disproportionately affects lower-income households, as they spend a larger portion of their income on essential goods like food and fuel. By keeping inflation in check, the RBI ensures that the purchasing power of these vulnerable groups is protected. For example, if food prices rise sharply, it can severely impact the poor, leading to higher levels of inequality. The RBI's focus on maintaining price stability helps create a stable economic environment, which is particularly beneficial for those at the bottom of the income pyramid.

The RBI also promotes inclusive growth through financial literacy and education initiatives. By raising awareness about banking services, credit facilities, and responsible borrowing, the central bank empowers individuals and small businesses to make informed financial decisions, leading to better financial health and economic participation.

In summary, through targeted lending policies, the expansion of financial services into underserved areas, inflation control, and financial literacy initiatives, the RBI ensures that the benefits of economic growth are shared more widely across different strata of society. This, in turn, contributes to a more inclusive and balanced economic development, where all citizens have the opportunity to participate in and benefit from the country's progress.

Overall, monetary policy plays a critical role in managing the Indian economy by maintaining price stability, promoting economic growth and ensuring financial stability.

E. TYPES OF MONETARY POLICIES

There are two main types of monetary policies: expansionary monetary policy and contractionary monetary policy.

1. Expansionary Monetary Policies:

Expansionary monetary policy refers to the actions taken by a central bank, such as the Reserve Bank of India (RBI), to stimulate economic growth by increasing the money supply and lowering interest rates. This type of policy is typically implemented during periods of economic slowdown or recession, where there is a need to boost spending, investment, and overall economic activity. The goal of expansionary monetary policy is to make borrowing cheaper, encouraging businesses to invest more and consumers to spend more, ultimately driving economic growth.

For example, if the economy is experiencing a slowdown, the RBI may lower the repo rate, which is the rate at which it lends money to commercial banks. A reduction in the repo rate means that banks can borrow money from the RBI at a lower cost. As a result, banks can offer loans to businesses and consumers at lower interest rates. This encourages businesses to take out loans to invest in new projects or expand operations, while consumers are more likely to borrow for purchasing homes or cars. The increased borrowing and spending help to stimulate demand in the economy, which can lead to higher production, job creation, and overall economic recovery.

Additionally, the RBI might use open market operations, buying government securities from the market to inject liquidity into the banking system. This increases the availability of funds in the economy, further promoting lending and investment. For example, during the global financial crisis of 2008, many central banks, including the RBI, adopted expansionary monetary policies to prevent deeper economic contractions by lowering interest rates and injecting liquidity into the financial system.

In summary, expansionary monetary policy is designed to boost economic activity by making money more accessible and cheaper to borrow. It is a critical tool used by central banks to counteract economic downturns and foster recovery.

2. Contraction Monetary Policies:

Contractionary monetary policy is the set of actions taken by a central bank, like the Reserve Bank of India (RBI), to reduce the money supply in the economy and increase interest rates in order to control inflation. This type of policy is typically implemented when the economy is growing too quickly, leading to rising prices or inflation. The main objective of contractionary monetary policy is to reduce excess demand, curb inflation, and maintain price stability, even if it means slowing down economic growth temporarily.

For instance, if inflation in India rises above the target level set by the RBI, the central bank might increase the repo rate, which is the rate at which it lends money to commercial banks. When the repo rate is raised, borrowing becomes more expensive for banks, which in turn makes loans more costly for businesses and consumers. As a result, there is less borrowing and spending, reducing demand in the economy. For example, if interest rates on home loans or car loans go up, consumers might delay purchasing homes or vehicles, which slows down demand in those sectors.

Another tool of contractionary monetary policy is selling government securities in open market operations. When the RBI sells these securities, it absorbs money from the banking system, reducing the liquidity available for banks to lend. With less money in circulation, banks become more cautious about offering loans, and businesses reduce their investments. This dampens overall spending in the economy, helping to bring inflation down.

For example, in the mid-2010s, when inflation was rising in India, the RBI used contractionary measures by raising the repo rate several times. This was aimed at cooling off the economy, reducing inflationary pressures, and ensuring that prices remained stable for consumers. Though these measures can slow economic growth, they are essential for keeping inflation under control and maintaining the long-term health of the economy.

In summary, contractionary monetary policy helps to control inflation by reducing the money supply and increasing interest rates, which in turn slows down spending and investment in the economy. While this may reduce economic growth in the short term, it is necessary to prevent runaway inflation and ensure stable economic conditions.

Both expansionary and contractionary monetary policies are used by central banks to maintain stability in the economy, control inflation, and support economic growth. The specific type of monetary policy used by a central bank will depend on the current state of the economy, its inflation and growth outlook, and other factors.

F. INSTRUMENTS OF MONETARY POLICY

Monetary policy is implemented by central banks through the use of various instruments. The most common instruments of monetary policy include:

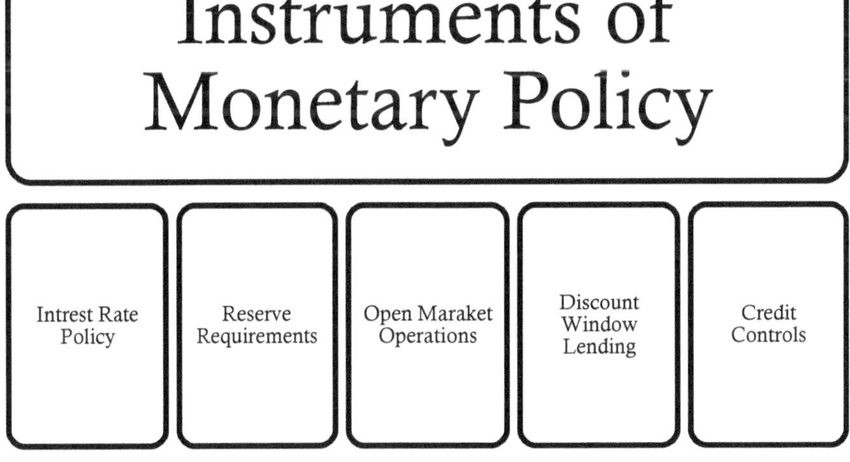

Exhibit 2.4: Instruments of Monetary Policy

1. Interest rate policy:

Central banks can influence interest rates by setting the policy rate, such as the repo rate, which is the rate at which banks can borrow money from the central bank.

A higher repo rate makes borrowing more expensive, reducing the money supply and slowing down economic activity, while a lower repo rate makes borrowing cheaper, increasing the money supply and stimulating economic activity.

2. Reserve requirements:

Central banks can require banks to hold a certain minimum level of reserves, which reduces the amount of money available for lending and can be used to control the money supply.

3. Open market operations:

Central banks can buy or sell government securities in the open market to inject or absorb liquidity, which influences the money supply.

4. Discount window lending:

Central banks can provide loans to commercial banks through the discount window, which is a lending facility provided by the central bank to banks.

5. Credit controls:

Central banks can implement credit controls, such as setting limits on the growth of certain types of lending, to control the money supply.

All these instruments are used to influence the money supply in the economy and implement monetary policy. The specific instruments used by a central bank will depend on the country's monetary policy objectives, the state of the economy, and other factors.

G. TYPES OF MONETARY POLICY INSTRUMENTS:

Quantitative Instruments of Monetary Policy

Quantitative instruments of monetary policy refer to the tools used by central banks to directly influence the money supply in an economy.

These tools are used to control the quantity of money in circulation and include:

1. Bank rate:

Bank rate is a monetary tool used by central banks, such as the Reserve Bank of India (RBI), to influence the cost of credit in the economy. The bank rate is the rate at which central banks provide loans to commercial banks, and changes in the bank rate will affect the cost of borrowing for banks and in turn influence the cost of credit for consumers and businesses.

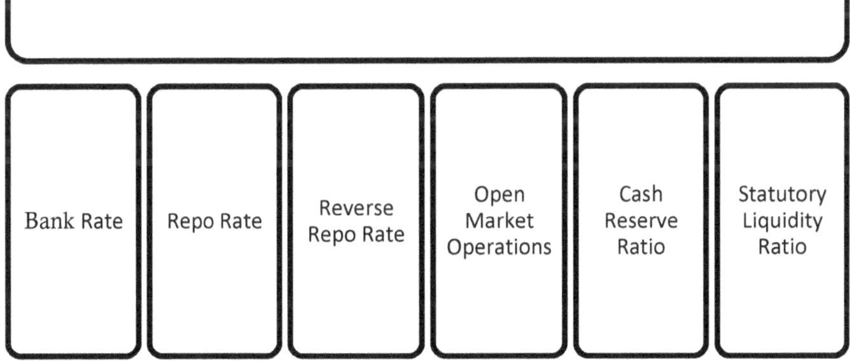

Exhibit 2.5: Quantitative Instruments of Monetary Policy

A higher bank rate makes borrowing more expensive, which reduces the money supply and slows down economic activity, while a lower bank rate makes borrowing cheaper, which increases the money supply and stimulates economic activity. By changing the bank rate, central banks can influence the level of spending and economic activity in the economy, and help maintain stability in the financial system.

Bank rate is an important monetary tool used by central banks to implement monetary policy and achieve their objectives, such as controlling inflation, supporting economic growth, and maintaining stability in the financial system.

2. Repo rate:

The repo rate is a monetary tool used by central banks, such as the Reserve Bank of India (RBI), to influence the cost of credit in the economy. The repo rate is the rate at which commercial banks can borrow money from the central bank by selling government securities, and it is a key policy rate set by the central bank.

A higher repo rate makes borrowing more expensive, which reduces the money supply and slows down economic activity, while a lower repo rate makes borrowing cheaper, which increases the money supply and stimulates economic activity. By changing the repo rate, central banks can influence the level of spending and economic activity in the economy, and help maintain stability in the financial system.

The repo rate is an important monetary tool used by central banks to implement monetary policy and achieve their objectives, such as controlling inflation, supporting economic growth, and maintaining stability in the financial system. Central banks use the repo rate to signal their stance on monetary policy, and changes in the repo rate are closely watched by financial markets and the public.

3. Reverse repo rate:

The reverse repo rate is a monetary tool used by central banks, such as the Reserve Bank of India (RBI), to influence the cost of borrowing for banks. The reverse repo rate is the rate at which commercial banks can lend money to the central bank, by purchasing government securities.

A higher reverse repo rate makes it more attractive for banks to lend money to the central bank, which takes money out of circulation and reduces the money supply, while a lower reverse repo rate makes it less attractive for banks to lend money to the central bank, which puts money back into circulation and increases the money supply.

The reverse repo rate is an important monetary tool used by central banks to manage short-term liquidity in the financial system, and to implement monetary policy and achieve their objectives, such as controlling inflation, supporting economic growth, and maintaining stability in the financial system. By adjusting the reverse repo rate, central banks can fine-tune their monetary policy and influence the cost and availability of credit in the economy.

4. Open market operations:

Open market operations (OMO) are a monetary tool used by central banks, such as the Reserve Bank of India (RBI), to directly influence the money supply in the economy. OMO involves the purchase or sale of government securities by the central bank in the open market, which affects the amount of money available for spending and economic activity.

When the central bank buys government securities, it injects money into the financial system, which increases the money supply and stimulates economic activity, while when it sells government securities, it absorbs money from the financial system, which reduces the money supply and slows down economic activity.

OMO is an important monetary tool used by central banks to implement monetary policy and achieve their objectives, such as controlling inflation, supporting economic growth, and maintaining stability in the financial system. By using OMO, central banks can quickly and effectively influence the money supply in the economy, and respond to changing economic conditions in real-time. OMO is widely used by central banks around the world as an effective monetary policy tool to achieve their objectives.

5. Cash reserve ratio:

The cash reserve ratio (CRR) is a monetary tool used by central banks, such as the Reserve Bank of India (RBI), to control the amount of money available for lending and spending in the economy. The CRR is the percentage of total deposits that commercial banks are required to keep with the central bank, and it acts as a reserve requirement that banks must maintain in order to be able to lend money.

A higher CRR reduces the amount of money available for lending and spending, which slows down economic activity, while a lower CRR increases the amount of money available for lending and spending, which stimulates economic activity. By adjusting the CRR, central banks can influence the money supply and the level of spending and economic activity in the economy.

The CRR is an important monetary tool used by central banks to implement monetary policy and achieve their objectives, such as controlling inflation, supporting economic growth, and maintaining stability in the financial system. By using the CRR, central banks can quickly and effectively regulate the amount of money available for lending and spending in the economy, and respond to changing economic conditions in real-time.

6. Statutory liquidity ratio:

The statutory liquidity ratio (SLR) is a monetary tool used by central banks, such as the Reserve Bank of India (RBI), to control the amount of money available for lending and spending in the economy. The SLR is the percentage of total deposits that commercial banks are required to hold in the form of liquid assets, such as government securities, gold, and other approved securities.

A higher SLR reduces the amount of money available for lending and spending, which slows down economic activity, while a lower

SLR increases the amount of money available for lending and spending, which stimulates economic activity. By adjusting the SLR, central banks can influence the money supply and the level of spending and economic activity in the economy.

The SLR is an important monetary tool used by central banks to implement monetary policy and achieve their objectives, such as controlling inflation, supporting economic growth, and maintaining stability in the financial system. By using the SLR, central banks can ensure that commercial banks have sufficient liquidity to meet the demands of their customers, and respond to changing economic conditions in real-time. The SLR also provides a cushion to the banking system in times of stress, by ensuring that banks have access to a minimum level of liquid assets to meet their obligations.

All these instruments directly affect the amount of money in circulation and the amount of money available for lending, which in turn affects the overall level of spending and economic activity in the economy. Quantitative instruments are particularly useful in situations where central banks need to quickly adjust the money supply, for example during periods of economic crisis or instability.

Qualitative Instruments of Monetary Policy

Qualitative instruments of monetary policy refer to the tools used by central banks to indirectly influence the money supply in an economy by affecting the cost and availability of credit.

These tools include:

1. Marginal requirements:

Marginal requirement, also known as the margin requirement, is a monetary tool used by central banks, such as the Reserve Bank of India (RBI), to control the amount of credit available in the economy. The margin requirement is the amount of collateral that must be posted by a borrower to secure a loan, and it acts as a limit on the amount of credit that can be extended.

A higher margin requirement reduces the amount of credit available for borrowing, which slows down economic activity, while a lower margin requirement increases the amount of credit available for borrowing, which stimulates economic activity. By adjusting the margin requirement, central banks can influence the amount of credit available in the economy and the level of spending and economic activity.

Marginal requirement is an important monetary tool used by central banks to implement monetary policy and achieve their objectives, such as controlling inflation, supporting economic growth, and maintaining stability in the financial system. By using the marginal requirement, central banks can regulate the amount of credit available in the economy, and respond to changing economic conditions in real-time. By requiring a higher margin, central banks can curb excessive borrowing and reduce the risk of asset bubbles and financial instability, while by lowering the margin requirement, they can encourage borrowing and support economic growth.

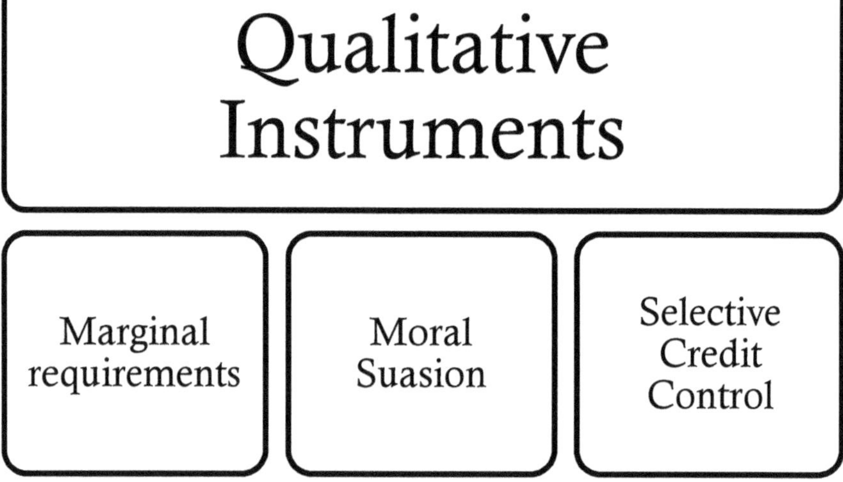

Exhibit 2.6: Qualitative Instruments of Monetary Policy

2. Moral suasion:

Moral suasion is a monetary tool used by central banks, such as the Reserve Bank of India (RBI), to influence the behavior of commercial banks and other financial institutions. Moral suasion refers to the use of persuasion, influence, and pressure by a central bank to encourage or discourage certain actions or behaviors by financial institutions.

For example, a central bank might use moral suasion to encourage commercial banks to lend more to certain sectors of the economy, such as small businesses, or to discourage them from lending to certain sectors that are perceived as risky or speculative.

Moral suasion is considered a soft monetary tool, as it does not involve the use of direct policy measures, such as changes in interest rates or reserve requirements, to control the money supply. Instead, it relies on the influence and credibility of the central bank to encourage financial institutions to follow a desired course of action.

Moral suasion is an important monetary tool used by central banks to implement monetary policy and achieve their objectives, such as controlling inflation, supporting economic growth, and maintaining stability in the financial system. By using moral suasion, central banks can communicate their expectations and encourage financial institutions to follow policies that are consistent with their objectives, without having to resort to more direct measures.

3. Selective credit control:

Selective credit control is a monetary tool used by central banks, such as the Reserve Bank of India (RBI), to control the supply of credit to specific sectors of the economy. Selective credit control is a targeted approach to monetary policy, where central banks use various instruments, such as interest rates, margin requirements, and reserve ratios, to regulate the flow of credit to specific sectors, such as agriculture, small businesses, or housing.

For example, a central bank might lower the interest rate for loans to small businesses, or increase the margin requirement for loans to the real estate sector, in order to encourage or discourage lending to those sectors.

Selective credit control is an important monetary tool used by central banks to implement monetary policy and achieve their objectives, such as controlling inflation, supporting economic growth, and maintaining stability in the financial system. By using selective credit control, central banks can regulate the flow of credit to specific sectors, and respond to changing economic conditions in real-time.

For example, if the central bank believes that the real estate sector is overheating and becoming a source of financial instability, it can use selective credit control measures to curb the flow of credit to that sector. Conversely, if the central bank wants to encourage lending to small businesses to support economic growth, it can use selective credit control measures to lower the cost of credit for those businesses.

Selective credit control can be a useful tool for central banks to balance their objectives of controlling inflation and supporting economic growth, and to ensure that the flow of credit is directed to sectors that can make the most productive use of it.

Qualitative instruments are particularly useful in situations where central banks want to fine-tune their monetary policy and target specific segments of the economy.

H. MEASUREMENT OF MONEY SUPPLY:

The Reserve Bank of India (RBI) measures the money supply in the Indian economy using various monetary aggregates, such as M0, M1, M2, M3, and M4.

M0: This is the narrowest definition of money supply and includes only currency in circulation and coins.

M1: This includes currency in circulation and demand deposits held in commercial banks.

M2: This includes M1 plus savings deposits held in commercial banks.

M3: This includes M2 plus time deposits held in commercial banks.

M4: This includes M3 plus long-term deposits held in commercial banks.

The RBI uses these measures of money supply to understand the growth and structure of the money supply in the Indian economy, and to assess the impact of its monetary policy on the economy. The RBI adjusts its monetary policy instruments, such as interest rates and open market operations, to influence the growth of the money supply and achieve its monetary policy objectives.

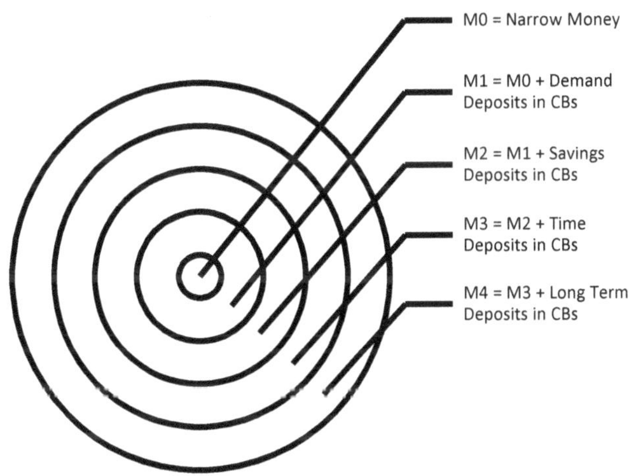

Exhibit 2.7: Measurement of Money Supply

For example, if the RBI wants to reduce inflation, it might use monetary policy tools to tighten the money supply and reduce the rate of growth of the money supply. Conversely, if the RBI wants to support economic growth, it might use monetary policy tools to loosen the money supply and increase the rate of growth of the money supply.

By monitoring and controlling the money supply, the RBI is able to influence economic activity, inflation, and financial stability in the Indian economy, and achieve its monetary policy objectives.

I. CHALLENGES FACED BY RBI IN CONTROL OF MONEY SUPPLY:

There are several challenges in controlling the money supply by the Reserve Bank of India (RBI), including:

1. Banks' Behaviour:

The RBI's ability to control the money supply is affected by the behavior of commercial banks. If banks decide to lend more or less, this can cause changes in the money supply that are beyond the control of the RBI.

2. Financial Innovation:

The development of new financial products and services can make it difficult for the RBI to accurately measure the money supply. For example, the growth of electronic payment systems and digital currencies can make it challenging to track the money supply in real-time.

3. Capital Flows:

The movement of capital in and out of the country can cause rapid changes in the money supply that are beyond the control of the RBI. For example, a large inflow of foreign investment can lead to an increase in the money supply, while a large outflow can lead to a decrease.

4. Inflation Targeting:

The RBI's focus on maintaining low inflation can sometimes conflict with its goal of controlling the money supply. If the RBI decides to tighten monetary policy to curb inflation, this can lead to a decrease in the money supply and slow economic growth.

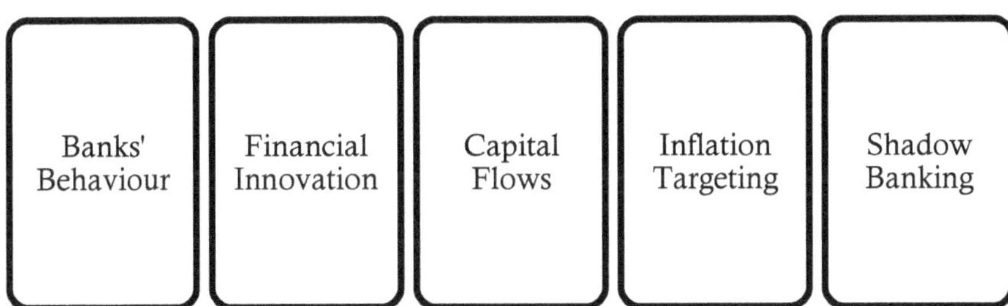

Exhibit 2.8: Challenges Faced by RBI in Control of Monetary Policy

5. Shadow Banking:

The growth of shadow banking can make it difficult for the RBI to control the money supply. Shadow banking refers to financial intermediaries that provide credit and other financial services outside of the regulated banking system. These activities can create liquidity risks and pose a threat to financial stability, making it challenging for the RBI to effectively control the money supply.

J. MONETARY POLICY COMMITTEE:

Section 45ZB of the amended RBI Act, 1934 provides for an empowered six-member monetary policy committee (MPC) to be constituted by the Central Government by notification in the Official Gazette.

The first such MPC was constituted on September 29, 2016.

The MPC determines the policy repo rate required to achieve the inflation target.

The MPC is required to meet at least four times in a year. The quorum for the meeting of the MPC is four members.

Each member of the MPC has one vote, and in the event of an equality of votes, the Governor has a second or casting vote.

Each Member of the Monetary Policy Committee writes a statement specifying the reasons for voting in favour of, or against the proposed resolution.

1. The Monetary policy process:

The Reserve Bank has notified Reserve Bank of India Monetary Policy Committee and Monetary Policy Process Regulations, 2016 which came into effect from August 01, 2016.

The Monetary Policy Process consists of the following:

a. Meeting schedule:

The schedule of monetary policy voting/decision meetings for the entire fiscal year is announced in advance.

b. Meeting notice:

Ordinarily, not less than fifteen days' notice is given to members for meetings of the Committee.

Should it be found necessary to convene an emergency meeting, 24 hours' notice is given to every member to enable him/her to attend, with technology enabled arrangements for even shorter notice period for meetings.

c. Meeting duration:

The duration of monetary policy meetings is as decided by the Committee.

The policy resolution is publicly released after the conclusion of the MPC meeting keeping in view the functioning and timing of financial markets.

The Reserve Bank's Monetary Policy Department (MPD) assists the MPC in formulating the monetary policy. The MPC in its meetings reviews the surveys conducted by the Reserve Bank to gauge consumer confidence, households' inflation expectations, corporate sector performance, credit conditions, the outlook for the industrial, services and infrastructure sectors, and the projections of professional forecasters.

The MPC also reviews in detail the staff's macroeconomic projections, and alternative scenarios around various risks to the outlook. Drawing on the above and after extensive discussions on the stance of monetary policy, the MPC adopts a resolution.

d. The MPC Resolution:

The Bank publishes, after the conclusion of every meeting of the MPC, the resolution adopted by the said Committee. The resolution includes the MPC's decision on the policy repo rate.

e. Minutes of the MPC meeting:

On the 14th day after every meeting of the MPC, the minutes of the proceedings of the MPC are published which include:

    i.   the resolution adopted by the MPC;

    ii.   the voting of each member on the resolution; and

    iii.   short written statements of individual members justifying the vote, consistent with the provisions of Section 45ZL of the RBI Act.

    iv.   Minutes shall be released at 5 pm on the 14th day from the date of the policy day (or next earliest working day, if a holiday in Mumbai).

f. The Monetary Policy Report:

Once in every six months, the Reserve Bank publishes the Monetary Policy Report containing the following elements:

i.   Explanation of inflation dynamics in the last six months and the near-term inflation outlook;

ii.   Projections of inflation and growth and the balance of risks;

iii.   An assessment of the state of the economy, covering the real economy, financial markets and stability, fiscal situation, and the external sector, which may entail a bearing on monetary policy decisions;

iv.   An updated review of the operating procedure of monetary policy; and

v.   An assessment of projection performance.

CHAPTER SUMMARY

MONETARY POLICY

The chapter on Monetary Policy explores the mechanisms through which the Reserve Bank of India (RBI) controls the money supply and maintains economic stability in India. It begins with an explanation of Monetary Policy in India, emphasizing its significance in regulating inflation, stabilizing the currency, and promoting sustainable economic growth.

The objectives of monetary policy in India are thoroughly discussed, highlighting the RBI's role in maintaining price stability, ensuring adequate credit flow to productive sectors, and fostering overall economic development. The chapter then details the RBI tools used to achieve these objectives, such as interest rate adjustments, open market operations, and reserve requirements.

A key focus of the chapter is the role of monetary policy in India, showcasing how it serves as a critical tool in balancing inflation and growth. The discussion of types of monetary policy—including expansionary and contractionary approaches—helps illustrate how the RBI either stimulates the economy or reins in inflationary pressures as needed.

The chapter also covers the instruments of monetary policy, such as the repo rate, reverse repo rate, and cash reserve ratio (CRR), explaining how these tools are used by the RBI to influence the economy. In addition, the chapter examines the measurement of money supply, highlighting how money supply indicators (like M1, M2, M3) are tracked and their importance in shaping policy decisions.

A significant portion of the chapter is devoted to the challenges faced by the RBI in controlling money supply, focusing on external shocks, fluctuating global markets, and the complexity of managing inflation in a growing economy. The role of the Monetary Policy Committee (MPC) is also introduced, explaining its critical function in setting interest rates and making policy decisions based on economic data and trends.

In summary, this chapter emphasizes the centrality of monetary policy in maintaining economic balance in India. It outlines the various objectives, tools, and instruments the RBI employs to manage inflation and economic growth while also shedding light on the challenges the central bank faces in achieving these goals. The chapter highlights the dynamic nature of monetary policy and its importance in steering India's economic trajectory.

CASE STUDIES

Case Study 2.1: RBI's Inflation Control through Monetary Policy (2013-2016)

Between 2013 and 2016, India faced high levels of inflation, primarily driven by rising food prices, oil prices, and a weakening rupee. The Reserve Bank of India (RBI), under the leadership of then-governor Raghuram Rajan, adopted a series of monetary policy measures to control inflation and stabilize the economy. This period saw a significant transformation in how the RBI managed inflation, moving towards an inflation-targeting framework for more effective control over price stability.

In 2013, inflation in India reached alarming levels, with consumer price inflation (CPI) hovering above 10%. This high inflation threatened to erode purchasing power and reduce the overall economic growth rate. The RBI, realizing that inflation control was critical for economic stability, employed its monetary policy tools to tighten liquidity in the market. The repo rate was raised multiple times during 2013-2014 to curb excessive money flow and reduce demand-side inflation pressures.

Under Rajan's leadership, the RBI also introduced a flexible inflation-targeting framework, which set a clear inflation target of 4% (with a 2% buffer on either side). This new policy framework, formalized in 2016 under the Monetary Policy Committee (MPC), became the RBI's key strategy to maintain price stability. The MPC, which includes both RBI officials and external experts, was tasked with deciding interest rates based on inflation forecasts and economic conditions.

In addition to raising interest rates, the RBI also worked to stabilize the rupee through its foreign exchange reserves, ensuring that external factors like rising crude oil prices and currency depreciation did not further aggravate inflation. The open market operations (OMOs) were used to manage liquidity and ensure that the tightening of monetary policy did not disrupt the banking system.

By mid-2016, the RBI's inflation-targeting framework proved to be effective, as inflation rates fell from double digits to around 5%. This success was attributed to the central bank's consistent focus on inflation management, even at the cost of short-term growth, demonstrating the effectiveness of monetary policy in maintaining price stability.

The case highlights the RBI's critical role in inflation control through monetary policy and showcases the importance of a targeted approach to price stability in fostering sustainable economic growth.

Questions Based on the Case:

i.   How did the RBI's use of monetary policy tools, such as changes in the repo rate, help control inflation during the period between 2013 and 2016?

ii.   What is the significance of the inflation-targeting framework introduced by the RBI, and how did the creation of the Monetary Policy Committee enhance this approach?

iii.   In what ways did external factors like oil prices and currency depreciation impact the RBI's inflation control measures, and how did the central bank address these challenges?

Case Study 2.2: Demonetization and its Impact on India's Monetary Policy (2016)

On November 8, 2016, the Government of India, in consultation with the Reserve Bank of India (RBI), announced the demonetization of ₹500 and ₹1,000 currency notes, which constituted around 86% of the currency in circulation at the time. The sudden withdrawal of these high-denomination notes aimed to curb black money, reduce corruption, and promote digital transactions. However, demonetization also posted significant challenges for the RBI in managing the monetary policy, especially in controlling liquidity and stabilizing the economy.

In the immediate aftermath of demonetization, there was a liquidity surplus in the banking system as people deposited their invalidated currency into banks. This influx of deposits increased the money supply, putting pressure on the RBI to take measures to prevent inflationary consequences. The central bank responded by utilizing several monetary policy instruments, such as reducing the cash reserve ratio (CRR), to absorb excess liquidity and control the money supply. The RBI also increased its use of reverse repo operations, whereby banks could park excess funds with the central bank, thereby reducing liquidity in the market.

Additionally, demonetization resulted in a temporary contraction in economic activity, particularly in cash-dependent sectors like agriculture, retail, and small businesses. This posed a challenge for the RBI as it needed to balance between managing liquidity and supporting economic recovery. To address this, the RBI lowered the repo rate in early 2017, making borrowing cheaper and providing a stimulus for economic growth. The central bank also closely monitored inflationary trends, as the liquidity crunch in the initial months helped lower inflation, which had been a major concern in previous years.

The long-term impact of demonetization on monetary policy was reflected in the RBI's renewed focus on digitization and formalization of the economy. Post-demonetization, the RBI promoted the use of digital payment platforms and facilitated greater integration of financial transactions within the formal banking system, which enhanced the transmission of monetary policy. Moreover, the reduction of cash transactions helped the RBI in achieving better control over the money supply and inflation.

Demonetization, while controversial, provided the RBI with an opportunity to refine its monetary policy tools and improve the mechanisms for controlling liquidity and inflation in the economy. It also underlined the importance of policy coordination between the central bank and the government in achieving broader economic objectives.

Questions Based on the Case:

i. How did the RBI manage the liquidity surplus in the banking system following demonetization, and what monetary policy instruments were used to control the money supply?

ii. What were the short-term and long-term impacts of demonetization on India's monetary policy, particularly concerning inflation and economic growth?

iii. How did demonetization influence the RBI's approach towards promoting digitization and the formalization of the Indian economy, and how did this shift impact monetary policy transmission?

Case Study 2.3: RBI's Response to COVID-19 Pandemic Through Monetary Policy (2020)

The outbreak of the COVID-19 pandemic in early 2020 presented an unprecedented challenge to economies worldwide, including India. The pandemic led to widespread disruptions in economic activities, a sharp decline in GDP, and a liquidity crisis across sectors. In response, the Reserve Bank of India (RBI) acted swiftly through its monetary policy to mitigate the economic impact, ensure financial stability, and provide relief to struggling businesses and households.

Recognizing the severity of the situation, the RBI took several bold steps to ease the strain on the economy. The first significant measure was an emergency reduction in the repo rate, the rate at which the RBI lends to commercial banks, by 75 basis points in March 2020, followed by further cuts later in the year. This drastic reduction aimed to lower borrowing costs for businesses and individuals, encouraging lending and economic activity at a time when both demand and supply were severely hit.

Additionally, the RBI introduced targeted long-term repo operations (TLTROs) to provide liquidity to specific sectors that were particularly affected by the pandemic, such as micro, small, and medium enterprises (MSMEs) and NBFCs. These measures ensured that banks could lend more freely to these sectors and help them survive the crisis. To address the immediate liquidity crunch in the market, the RBI also reduced the cash reserve ratio (CRR) for banks, allowing them to have more funds at their disposal for lending and managing operations.

Furthermore, the central bank announced a loan moratorium for a six-month period, providing relief to borrowers who were facing cash flow constraints due to lockdowns and the economic slowdown. This moratorium allowed businesses and individuals to defer loan repayments without it impacting their credit scores, giving them time to stabilize financially.

The RBI's monetary policy response was complemented by a host of other measures, such as reducing the reverse repo rate to discourage banks from parking excess funds with the RBI and instead lend more actively in the economy. The central bank also engaged in open market operations (OMOs) and purchased government securities to inject liquidity into the financial system. This helped maintain financial stability during a period of heightened uncertainty.

By the end of 2020, while the pandemic was still ongoing, the RBI's proactive stance through its monetary policy had managed to cushion the economic blow, restore liquidity, and support recovery efforts. The measures taken were crucial in stabilizing the financial system and aiding in the early stages of economic recovery.

Questions Based on the Case:

i. How did the RBI's monetary policy response to the COVID-19 pandemic help in mitigating the economic challenges posed by the crisis, particularly in terms of liquidity and credit availability?

ii.   What role did the reduction in the repo rate and the introduction of TLTROs play in supporting specific sectors, such as MSMEs and NBFCs, during the pandemic?

iii.   How effective was the loan moratorium in providing relief to borrowers, and what were the potential long-term impacts of this measure on the banking sector and monetary policy?

Case Study 2.4: The RBI's Role in Tackling the 2018 NBFC Liquidity Crisis

In 2018, the Indian financial system faced a serious liquidity crunch due to the Non-Banking Financial Companies (NBFCs) crisis, triggered by the default of Infrastructure Leasing & Financial Services (IL&FS). IL&FS, a major player in the infrastructure financing space, defaulted on its debt obligations, which led to a severe liquidity shortage across the NBFC sector. This crisis raised concerns about financial stability, as many NBFCs played a crucial role in providing credit to sectors such as housing, automobiles, and microfinance.

The Reserve Bank of India (RBI) acted swiftly to prevent the situation from escalating into a full-blown financial crisis. The central bank adopted a range of monetary policy measures to ensure adequate liquidity in the system and restore confidence among financial institutions and market participants.

One of the key measures was an increase in open market operations (OMOs) to inject liquidity into the banking system. The RBI purchased government securities worth billions to ensure that banks had sufficient liquidity to lend to NBFCs and other sectors affected by the crisis. This was particularly important as many NBFCs relied on short-term borrowing to meet their obligations, and the lack of liquidity in the market made it difficult for them to roll over their debt.

In addition to OMOs, the RBI also allowed banks to provide additional credit to NBFCs through the Liquidity Coverage Ratio

(LCR) adjustment. This permitted banks to hold lower liquid assets temporarily, enabling them to lend more to NBFCs that were facing liquidity stress. Furthermore, the RBI encouraged bank-NBFC partnerships to ensure that credit continued to flow to sectors like housing finance and small businesses, which were highly dependent on NBFC funding.

Another important step taken by the RBI was the establishment of a special NBFC liquidity window, allowing banks to extend longer-term loans to well-performing NBFCs, thereby ensuring their survival and preventing further defaults in the sector. The central bank also closely monitored the exposure of banks to NBFCs to ensure that the crisis did not spread into the banking sector.

While the liquidity crisis exposed structural weaknesses in the NBFC sector, the RBI's monetary policy interventions were critical in managing the situation. By ensuring sufficient liquidity and encouraging greater oversight of NBFCs, the RBI helped stabilize the financial system and prevent a contagion effect that could have impacted the broader economy.

Questions Based on the Case:

i. How did the RBI use open market operations (OMOs) and other monetary policy tools to address the liquidity crisis faced by NBFCs in 2018?

ii. What was the impact of the IL&FS default on the NBFC sector, and how did the RBI ensure that the crisis did not spread to other financial institutions?

iii. How did the RBI's measures help in restoring confidence in the financial system, particularly in relation to the NBFC sector's role in lending to key economic sectors?

OPEN MARKET OPERATIONS

Learning Objectives:

- *Understand what open market operations are and their role in controlling the money supply in the economy.*
- *Learn how the Reserve Bank of India (RBI) uses open market operations to buy and sell government securities to manage inflation and liquidity.*
- *Explore the different types of government securities used in open market operations in India.*
- *Understand the importance of open market operations in maintaining economic stability and controlling inflation.*
- *Identify the challenges the RBI faces when conducting open market operations, such as managing market reactions and balancing money supply.*
- *Learn about key monetary ratios and their connection to*

OPEN MARKET OPERATIONS

Open market operations (OMO) refer to the purchase or sale of government securities in the open market by a central bank, with the goal of influencing the money supply and, ultimately, achieving its monetary policy objectives. By buying securities, the central bank injects money into the banking system, thereby increasing the money supply, while selling securities reduces the money supply by absorbing excess liquidity in the banking system. This is one of the primary tools used by central banks to regulate the economy.

A. FUNCTIONS OF OPEN MARKET OPERATIONS

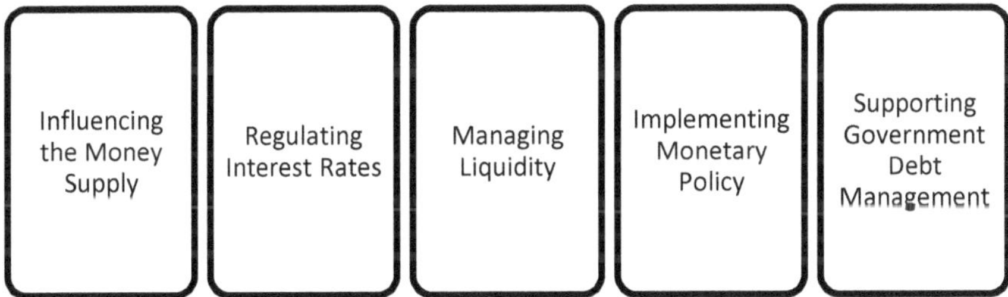

Exhibit 3.1: Functions of Open Market Operations

1. Influencing the money supply:

Open market operations allow central banks to control the amount of money in circulation, thereby affecting economic activity and inflation.

2. Regulating interest rates:

By adjusting the supply of money, open market operations can influence short-term interest rates, which, in turn, affects long-term rates and borrowing costs for households and businesses.

3. Managing liquidity:

Central banks can use open market operations to manage the banking system's overall liquidity, ensuring that banks have enough reserves to meet their obligations and maintain stability.

4. Implementing monetary policy:

Open market operations are a crucial tool for central banks to implement their monetary policy objectives, such as controlling inflation and promoting economic growth.

5. Supporting government debt management:

Central banks can also use open market operations to support the government's debt management strategy by buying or selling government securities.

In summary, open market operations play a key role in central banks' efforts to maintain price stability, promote economic growth, and maintain financial stability.

B. MONETARY RATIOS

Monetary ratios refer to a set of numerical values that central banks use to measure various aspects of the money supply, credit, and financial system. These ratios help central banks to monitor and evaluate the effectiveness of their monetary policies, assess the stability of the financial system, and identify emerging risks and imbalances.

These monetary ratios provide central banks with a comprehensive view of the financial system and help them make informed decisions on monetary policy.

1. M1:

M1 is a measure of the money supply that includes currency in circulation (i.e., physical currency, including coins and banknotes) and demand deposits (i.e., checking accounts that allow for immediate access to funds).

M1 is considered a narrow measure of the money supply as it only includes the most liquid forms of money, which can be used for immediate transactions.

M1 is important for central banks and economists because it provides a snapshot of the amount of money that is readily available for spending in the economy.

Changes in M1 can provide early signals of changes in economic activity and inflation, as an increase in M1 usually leads to increased spending and vice versa.

Central banks often use changes in M1 as an indicator of the effectiveness of their monetary policy decisions and to determine the need for further policy actions.

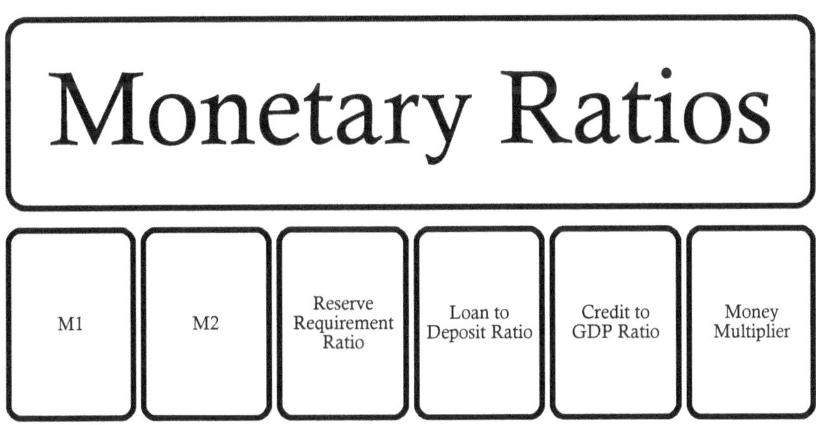

Exhibit 3.2: Monetary Ratios

2. M2:

M2 is a broader measure of the money supply that includes all the components of M1, as well as "near money," which are savings deposits, time deposits (such as certificates of deposit), and money market securities with maturities of less than one year.

M2 is considered a more inclusive measure of the money supply than M1, as it captures not only the most liquid forms of money, but also fewer liquid forms that can be used for transactions and savings purposes.

M2 provides a more complete picture of the money supply in an economy, as it includes not only the funds that are readily available for spending, but also the funds that are less accessible but still contribute to spending power.

This makes M2 a useful tool for central banks to assess the overall health of the economy, as well as the demand for money and credit.

Like M1, changes in M2 can also provide early signals of changes in economic activity and inflation, and central banks may use changes in M2 to inform their monetary policy decisions.

However, M2 is generally considered to be a less reliable indicator of economic activity and inflation than M1, as changes in M2 can be influenced by factors such as changes in savings and investment behavior.

3. Reserve Requirement Ratio:

The reserve requirement ratio (RRR) is the percentage of deposits that banks are required to hold in reserve as cash or deposits with their central bank.

This ratio is set by the central bank and can vary depending on the economic conditions and policy objectives.

The reserve requirement ratio is used by central banks as a tool to regulate the amount of money that banks can lend out as loans, thereby affecting the money supply and credit conditions in the economy.

A higher reserve requirement ratio means that banks have less money to lend out, which can reduce the money supply and credit growth, while a lower reserve requirement ratio means that banks have more money to lend out, which can stimulate economic activity and credit growth.

Central banks can adjust the reserve requirement ratio as a part of their monetary policy toolkit to achieve their policy objectives, such as controlling inflation or promoting economic growth.

By increasing or decreasing the reserve requirement ratio, the central bank can influence the amount of money in circulation and the overall liquidity of the financial system.

4. Loan to Deposit Ratio

The loan-to-deposit (LTD) ratio is a financial ratio that expresses the amount of loans that a bank has issued relative to the number of deposits it has received from customers.

It is calculated by dividing a bank's total loans outstanding by its total customer deposits.

The loan-to-deposit ratio is an important indicator of a bank's lending and liquidity risk.

A high loan-to-deposit ratio indicates that the bank is relying heavily on customer deposits to fund its lending activities and may have limited liquidity to meet unexpected withdrawals or loan losses.

A low loan-to-deposit ratio may indicate that the bank is being overly conservative and may not be maximizing its potential profitability.

The loan-to-deposit ratio is also closely monitored by regulators and policymakers as a measure of the health and stability of the banking system.

A high LTD ratio across the banking system may indicate that the financial system is vulnerable to liquidity or solvency risks, while a low LTD ratio may indicate that banks are not lending enough to support economic growth.

In summary, the loan-to-deposit ratio is a useful tool for banks, regulators, and policymakers to monitor the balance between lending and liquidity, and to assess the health and stability of the banking system.

5. Credit to GDP Ratio:

The credit-to-GDP ratio is a financial ratio that measures the amount of credit in an economy relative to the size of the economy, as measured by its gross domestic product (GDP).

It is calculated by dividing the total amount of credit provided by the banking sector in a given period by the country's GDP for the same period.

The credit-to-GDP ratio is an important indicator of the level of credit in an economy and its potential impact on economic growth and financial stability.

A high credit-to-GDP ratio may indicate that the level of debt in the economy is becoming unsustainable and may lead to financial instability and economic imbalances.

On the other hand, a low credit-to-GDP ratio may indicate that credit is not being used efficiently to support economic growth and development.

The credit-to-GDP ratio is closely monitored by central banks and other regulators to identify potential risks and imbalances in the financial system.

In general, a credit-to-GDP ratio of around 100% is considered a reasonable benchmark for a healthy and stable financial system.

However, the appropriate level of the credit-to-GDP ratio may vary depending on the specific characteristics of the economy, such as its stage of development, financial deepening, and structural features.

In summary, the credit-to-GDP ratio is a useful tool for assessing the level and impact of credit in an economy and identifying potential risks and imbalances in the financial system.

6. Money Multiplier:

The money multiplier is a concept in economics that measures the potential increase in the money supply through the creation of new bank deposits.

It represents the amount by which the money supply can increase from an initial injection of funds into the banking system, assuming that banks hold only the required reserve ratio and lend out the remaining funds.

The money multiplier formula is calculated as the reciprocal of the required reserve ratio. For example, if the required reserve ratio is 10%, the money multiplier would be $1/0.1$, or 10.

This means that an initial injection of $1 billion into the banking system could potentially lead to a $10 billion increase in the money supply, assuming that banks lend out all the excess reserves and there are no leakages from the system.

However, in reality, the money multiplier is not a fixed or constant ratio, as there are many factors that can affect the lending behavior of banks and the behavior of households and businesses. For example, if banks are reluctant to lend due to uncertainty or risk aversion, the money multiplier may be smaller than expected. Conversely, if households and businesses are eager to borrow, the money multiplier may be larger than expected.

Despite these limitations, the money multiplier concept remains a useful tool for understanding the relationship between the money supply, bank reserves, and bank lending.

It is also an important concept in monetary policy, as central banks can use changes in the required reserve ratio or other policy tools to influence the money multiplier and the overall money supply in the economy.

C. TYPES OF GOVERNMENT SECURITIES IN OPEN MARKET IN INDIA

The Reserve Bank of India (RBI) conducts open market operations (OMOs) to buy or sell these government securities in the open market to influence the liquidity and interest rate conditions in the economy. By buying government securities, the RBI injects liquidity into the system, while selling them withdraws liquidity from the system.

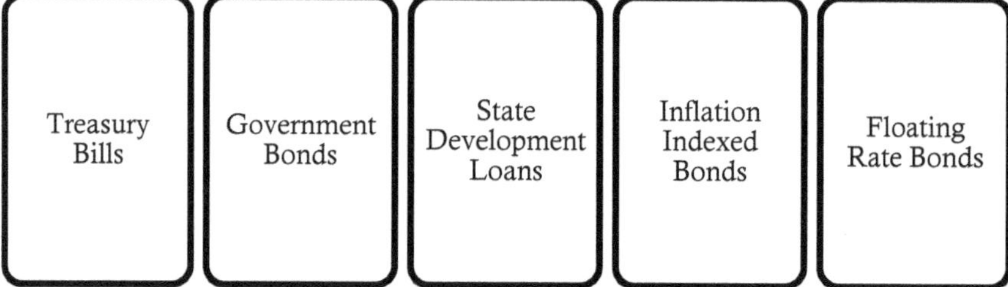

Exhibit 3.3: Types of Government Securities in Open Market Operations

In India, the government issues several types of securities that can be traded in the open market.

These include:

1. Treasury Bills:

In India, Treasury Bills (T-Bills) are short-term debt instruments issued by the central government through the Reserve Bank of India (RBI) on a regular basis to meet its short-term funding requirements.

T-Bills are one of the safest forms of investment as they are backed by the credit of the Indian government. These are issued at a discount to the face value and mature at face value, which means that the investor earns the difference between the purchase price and the face value at maturity.

The maturity period of T-Bills ranges from 91 days, 182 days, and 364 days. The 91-day and 182-day T-Bills are auctioned every week, while the 364-day T-Bill is auctioned every alternate week.

T-Bills are a popular investment option for individuals, banks, and other financial institutions as they offer a low-risk investment with a fixed return. They are also a preferred investment option for banks to meet their statutory liquidity ratio (SLR) requirements, as they are considered as an approved form of investment under the SLR guidelines.

Investors can buy T-Bills through banks, primary dealers, or through the RBI's auction process. The auction process involves submitting bids through an electronic platform, and the allotment of T-Bills is done on a competitive or non-competitive basis. The competitive bidders bid at a discount to the face value, while the non-competitive bidders bid at the cut-off price decided by the RBI.

Overall, T-Bills are an important component of the Indian government's borrowing program and provide a safe and low-risk investment option to investors while also contributing to the management of liquidity in the financial system.

2. Government Bonds:

In India, government bonds are long-term debt instruments issued by the central government to raise funds for its various development and expenditure programs. These bonds are considered to be low-risk investments as they are backed by the credit of the Indian government.

Government bonds have a fixed coupon rate, which is the interest rate paid to the bondholder at regular intervals until the bond's maturity. They are typically issued with a maturity of 5 years, 10 years, 15 years, or 20 years, and the interest rate on these bonds varies depending on the prevailing market conditions and the tenure of the bond.

In India, government bonds are traded on the National Stock Exchange (NSE) and the Bombay Stock Exchange (BSE), as well as over the counter (OTC) markets. They can be bought and sold in the secondary market through brokers, financial institutions, or through online trading platforms.

Investing in government bonds is considered to be a safe and low-risk investment option, especially for those investors who are risk-averse and looking for a regular income stream. However, the returns on government bonds are typically lower compared to other investment options such as equities or mutual funds.

3. State Development Loans

In India, State Development Loans (SDLs) are debt securities issued by state governments to raise funds for financing their development projects and other expenditures. These are long-term debt instruments with a maturity period of up to 10 years and are issued through an auction process conducted by the Reserve Bank of India (RBI).

SDLs are similar to government bonds issued by the central government but are issued by state governments. They are also considered to be low-risk investments as they are backed by the credit of the respective state government.

The interest rate on SDLs is generally higher compared to government bonds as the credit rating of state governments is usually lower than that of the central government. The interest rate on SDLs is determined through the auction process conducted by the RBI, where bidders can bid for the bonds at a price equal to or higher than the minimum bid yield fixed by the RBI.

SDLs can be bought and sold in the secondary market through brokers or financial institutions. They are typically traded at a premium or a discount to their face value depending on the prevailing market conditions and the interest rate environment.

Investing in SDLs can provide investors with a stable and regular income stream as they pay a fixed rate of interest at regular intervals. SDLs are also considered to be an attractive investment option for banks and financial institutions to meet their statutory liquidity ratio (SLR) requirements, as they are considered as an approved form of investment under the SLR guidelines.

Overall, SDLs are an important source of funding for state governments to finance their development projects and other expenditures while also providing investors with a safe and attractive investment option.

4. Inflation-Indexed Bonds

Inflation-indexed bonds (IIBs) are a type of government bond in India that provides investors with protection against inflation. These bonds are issued by the Reserve Bank of India (RBI) on behalf of the government and are designed to offer a real rate of return that keeps pace with inflation.

IIBs have a fixed coupon rate, like traditional bonds, but the principal value and interest payments are adjusted for changes in the inflation rate. The principal value is adjusted every six months based on the consumer price index (CPI) inflation rate, while the interest payments are adjusted every six months based on the adjusted principal value.

Investing in IIBs can be beneficial for investors looking for a low-risk investment option that provides protection against inflation. These bonds offer a fixed real rate of return that is immune to inflationary pressures, making them a good hedge against inflation.

IIBs can also be a good investment option for risk-averse investors who want to invest in government bonds but are concerned about the impact of inflation on their investment returns.

IIBs are available in different maturities, ranging from 5 years to 40 years. They are typically issued through an auction process, and investors can bid for these bonds at a price equal to or higher than the minimum bid yield fixed by the RBI.

IIBs can also be traded in the secondary market through brokers and financial institutions.

Overall, IIBs are an attractive investment option for investors looking for a low-risk investment with a fixed real rate of return that protects against inflation. These bonds are an important component of the government's borrowing program and contribute to the development of the bond market in India.

5. Floating Rate Bonds

Floating rate bonds are a type of debt security in India that offer a variable interest rate. These bonds have an interest rate that is adjusted periodically based on a benchmark rate such as the repo rate or the treasury bill rate.

As the benchmark rate changes, the interest rate on the bond changes as well. Floating rate bonds are issued by the government, as well as by public and private sector companies. They are typically issued with a maturity of 3 to 5 years and can be bought and sold in the secondary market through brokers or financial institutions.

Investing in floating rate bonds can be beneficial for investors who are looking for a fixed income investment option that can provide protection against interest rate fluctuations. Since the interest rate on floating rate bonds is adjusted periodically, the bond's value is less sensitive to changes in interest rates, making it less risky compared to traditional fixed rate bonds.

Floating rate bonds are an important source of funding for government and corporate entities, and they provide an opportunity for these entities to access capital at a lower cost than traditional fixed-rate bonds.

Investors in floating rate bonds receive a variable rate of interest that reflects the prevailing interest rate environment, providing a return that adjusts to changes in the economy.

Overall, floating rate bonds are an attractive investment option for investors looking for a low-risk investment with a fixed income component that provides protection against interest rate risk. These bonds are an important component of the Indian bond market and contribute to the development of the financial system in India.

D. FEATURES AND SIGNIFICANCE OF OPEN MARKET OPERATIONS

Open market operations (OMOs) are one of the primary tools used by central banks, such as the Reserve Bank of India (RBI), to implement monetary policy. OMOs involve the purchase or sale of government securities in the open market, with the aim of influencing the level of liquidity in the financial system and the level of interest rates.

Some key features and significance of OMOs are:

1. Flexibility:

OMOs are a flexible tool that can be used to fine-tune monetary policy based on the prevailing economic conditions. The RBI can adjust the size and timing of its OMOs to achieve its desired policy objectives.

2. Precision:

OMOs can be precisely targeted to impact specific segments of the financial system or particular interest rates. This precision allows the RBI to achieve its policy objectives without affecting the overall economy.

3. Transparency:

The RBI publishes details of its OMOs on its website, which makes the policy more transparent and helps market participants understand the central bank's policy objectives.

4. Market-driven:

OMOs are market-driven operations that rely on the supply and demand for government securities in the open market. This makes the policy more responsive to market conditions and helps ensure that the policy is effective.

5. Significance:

OMOs have a significant impact on the level of liquidity in the financial system and the level of interest rates. By increasing or decreasing the supply of government securities, the RBI can influence the cost of borrowing and the level of economic activity in the country.

In summary, open market operations are a flexible, precise, transparent, and market-driven tool that central banks, such as the RBI, use to implement monetary policy. By influencing the level of liquidity in the financial system and the level of interest rates, OMOs can have a significant impact on the economy, making them an essential tool for central banks.

Other factors effecting monetary base and bank reserves:

Apart from open market operations, there are several other factors that can impact the monetary base and bank reserves.

Here are some of the key factors in more detail:

1. Government transactions:

Transactions by the government, such as tax collections and government spending, can impact the monetary base and bank reserves.

When the government collects taxes, it reduces the amount of money in circulation, which can reduce bank reserves. Conversely, when the government spends money, it can increase bank reserves. For example, when the government spends money on infrastructure projects, it can lead to an increase in bank reserves as the contractors receive payment and deposit the money in banks.

2. Foreign exchange transactions:

Foreign exchange transactions, such as the purchase or sale of foreign currencies by the central bank, can impact the monetary base and bank reserves.

For example, if the RBI sells foreign currency, it can reduce bank reserves as the banks exchange rupees for the foreign currency. Similarly, if the RBI buys foreign currency, it can increase bank reserves as the banks receive rupees in exchange for the foreign currency.

3. Changes in reserve requirements:

Changes in the reserve requirement ratio, which is the percentage of deposits that banks must hold as reserves, can impact bank reserves. If the RBI increases the reserve requirement ratio, it can reduce bank reserves, while a decrease in the ratio can increase bank reserves.

For example, if the reserve requirement ratio is 10%, a bank with deposits of Rs. 1,000 crores must hold Rs. 100 crores as reserves. If the RBI increases the ratio to 12%, the same bank must hold Rs. 120 crores as reserves, which reduces its available reserves.

4. Lending and borrowing by banks:

Lending and borrowing by banks can impact bank reserves. When banks lend money, it can reduce their reserves, while borrowing can increase their reserves.

For example, when a bank lends Rs. 100 crores to a customer, it reduces its reserves as the money leaves the bank's account. Conversely, when a bank borrows money from the RBI, it increases its reserves as it receives the borrowed money in its account.

5. Non-bank financial institutions:

Non-bank financial institutions, such as mutual funds and insurance companies, can impact bank reserves. When these institutions invest in government securities or deposit their funds in banks, it can increase bank reserves.

For example, if a mutual fund invests Rs. 1,000 crores in government securities, it increases the demand for these securities and can lead to an increase in their price. This, in turn, can increase the value of the bank's holdings of these securities and hence its reserves.

In summary, several factors can impact the monetary base and bank reserves, in addition to open market operations. These factors can be both internal and external to the banking system, and the RBI needs to monitor them closely to ensure that monetary policy objectives are achieved.

E. CHALLENGES FACED BY RBI FOR CONDUCTING OPEN MARKET OPERATIONS

The Reserve Bank of India (RBI) faces several challenges when conducting open market operations (OMOs). Some of the key challenges are:

1. Market conditions:

The effectiveness of OMOs can be affected by market conditions, such as liquidity conditions, demand and supply dynamics, and investor sentiment. The RBI needs to monitor these conditions and adjust its operations accordingly to achieve its desired policy objectives.

2. Fiscal constraints:

The RBI's ability to conduct OMOs can be constrained by the government's fiscal position. In a situation where the government is running a large fiscal deficit, it may issue a large number of bonds, which can reduce the effectiveness of OMOs.

3. Interest rate volatility:

Interest rate volatility can make it difficult for the RBI to conduct OMOs. If interest rates are highly volatile, market participants may be hesitant to buy government securities, which can affect the RBI's ability to carry out its OMOs.

4. Lack of market depth:

The depth of the Indian bond market is limited, which can make it difficult for the RBI to conduct OMOs. The RBI may need to purchase or sell a large number of securities to achieve its desired policy objectives, but if there is a lack of market depth, this can be challenging.

5. Communication:

The RBI needs to effectively communicate its policy intentions to market participants to ensure that OMOs are carried out smoothly. If market participants are unclear about the RBI's policy objectives, this can lead to volatility in the bond market, making it difficult for the RBI to conduct its operations effectively.

In summary, the RBI faces several challenges when conducting open market operations, and it needs to be vigilant and proactive in addressing these challenges to ensure that its policy objectives are achieved.

CHAPTER SUMMARY

OPEN MARKET OPERATIONS

The chapter on Open Market Operations provides an in-depth exploration of how the Reserve Bank of India (RBI) uses open market operations (OMOs) as a vital tool to regulate liquidity in the economy and control the money supply. It begins by explaining the functions of open market operations, focusing on how the RBI buys and sells government securities in the open market to influence the availability of money and credit in the banking system.

The chapter then elaborates on monetary ratios, which include various economic indicators that are crucial in determining the RBI's strategy when conducting OMOs. It also describes the types of government securities involved in these operations, ranging from Treasury Bills to long-term government bonds, and how they are utilized to either inject or absorb liquidity.

The features and significance of open market operations are discussed at length, highlighting their importance in stabilizing interest rates, controlling inflation, and ensuring smooth functioning of the financial markets. The chapter points out that OMOs serve as a key mechanism through which the RBI maintains control over short-term interest rates, helping to guide economic activity and keep inflation within acceptable bounds.

Moreover, the chapter addresses the challenges faced by the RBI in conducting open market operations, such as fluctuations in global financial markets, changing macroeconomic conditions, and managing the trade-off between liquidity control and fostering economic growth. These challenges underscore the complexity of using OMOs as an effective policy tool in a rapidly evolving financial landscape.

In conclusion, this chapter underscores the strategic importance of open market operations in regulating India's monetary environment. Through the buying and selling of government securities, the RBI is able to influence liquidity levels, stabilize interest rates, and maintain financial market stability. However, the challenges the RBI faces in executing these operations are significant, requiring careful planning and execution to achieve the desired economic outcomes.

CASE STUDIES

Case Study 3.1: RBI's Open Market Operations to Stabilize the Rupee (2018)

In 2018, the Indian economy faced significant challenges due to a sharp depreciation of the Indian rupee (INR) against the US dollar. External factors, such as the rising price of crude oil and the tightening of monetary policy by the US Federal Reserve, triggered capital outflows from emerging markets, including India. As a result, the rupee depreciated, reaching an all-time low of INR 74 per USD by October 2018. This situation prompted the Reserve Bank of India (RBI) to intervene through Open Market Operations (OMOs) to manage liquidity and stabilize the currency.

The RBI's primary tool for tackling the situation was the sale of government securities in the open market. By selling these securities, the central bank aimed to absorb excess liquidity from the banking system, which would reduce the supply of rupees and curb the currency's depreciation. Throughout 2018, the RBI conducted multiple rounds of OMOs, where it cumulatively sold over ₹1.5 lakh crore worth of government bonds. This was one of the largest OMO interventions conducted by the RBI in recent times.

The objective of these OMOs was two-fold: first, to stabilize the rupee by reducing liquidity, and second, to ensure that inflationary pressures did not worsen due to rising import costs, particularly for oil, which had a direct impact on the economy. The sale of securities also indirectly impacted the bond market, as yields on government bonds increased due to higher demand for liquidity, which made borrowing more expensive for the government and other borrowers in the financial market.

In addition to OMOs, the RBI raised interest rates to further support the rupee and attract foreign capital inflows, which had been declining. The central bank's actions helped to stabilize the currency, and by the end of the year, the rupee had recovered to a more stable range. The RBI's OMO strategy, combined with interest rate hikes, helped mitigate the impact of external shocks on the Indian economy and ensured financial stability during a period of heightened global volatility.

Questions Based on the Case:

i. How did the RBI's open market operations (OMOs) help in absorbing excess liquidity and stabilizing the Indian rupee during the 2018 depreciation crisis?

ii. What were the direct and indirect impacts of the RBI's sale of government securities on the Indian bond market and overall economy?

iii. In what ways did external factors, such as global oil prices and US monetary policy, influence the RBI's decision to intervene through OMOs?

Case Study 3.2: RBI's Open Market Operations During the COVID-19 Pandemic (2020)

In 2020, the COVID-19 pandemic caused severe disruptions to the global economy, including India's financial markets. The pandemic led to a sharp economic contraction, a significant drop in consumer demand, and major liquidity stress across various sectors. As the economy went into lockdown, businesses faced cash flow problems, which had a ripple effect on the banking system and financial markets. In response, the Reserve Bank of India (RBI) undertook a series of Open Market Operations (OMOs) to inject liquidity into the system and prevent a financial meltdown.

One of the key interventions was the RBI's purchase of government securities through OMOs, which provided much-needed liquidity to the banking sector. By purchasing government bonds, the RBI injected billions of rupees into the system, ensuring that banks had adequate cash reserves to continue lending to businesses and individuals during the crisis. This move was crucial in maintaining the flow of credit to sectors that were severely affected by the pandemic, such as manufacturing, retail, and small businesses.

In addition to regular OMOs, the RBI also introduced Targeted Long-Term Repo Operations (TLTROs), a special liquidity measure aimed at directing funds to specific sectors of the economy that were in dire need of credit. Under this scheme, the RBI provided liquidity to banks at a low interest rate on the condition that they would lend the money to businesses in stressed sectors, such as Non-Banking Financial Companies (NBFCs) and Micro, Small, and Medium Enterprises (MSMEs). This innovative use of OMOs helped ensure that liquidity reached the parts of the economy that were most in need, without inflating asset prices unnecessarily.

Another critical measure taken by the RBI was Operation Twist, where the central bank conducted simultaneous buying and selling of government securities to manage the yield curve. By purchasing long-term bonds and selling short-term bonds, the RBI aimed to reduce long-term interest rates, making it cheaper for businesses to borrow for investments and recovery while managing the short-term liquidity situation.

These OMO interventions helped stabilize financial markets, ensuring that businesses had access to the credit they needed to survive the pandemic. The RBI's actions helped mitigate the worst effects of the economic contraction, maintained market confidence, and played a key role in preventing a deeper financial crisis during one of the most challenging periods in recent history.

Questions Based on the Case:

i. How did the RBI's use of open market operations (OMOs) during the COVID-19 pandemic ensure sufficient liquidity in the financial system?

ii. What was the role of Targeted Long-Term Repo Operations (TLTROs) in directing liquidity to specific sectors of the economy during the crisis?

iii.   How did the RBI's use of Operation Twist impact long-term borrowing costs and the overall recovery of businesses during the pandemic?

Case Study 3.3: Impact of RBI's Open Market Operations on the Indian Bond Market (2019)

In 2019, the Indian economy faced several challenges, including a slowdown in GDP growth, weak demand in key sectors, and a stressed banking sector. To stimulate growth and manage liquidity, the Reserve Bank of India (RBI) intensified its use of Open Market Operations (OMOs), focusing particularly on the Indian bond market. The central bank's goal was to ensure that the banking system had adequate liquidity while simultaneously keeping interest rates at manageable levels to support economic growth.

One of the most significant OMO actions taken by the RBI in 2019 was the large-scale purchase of government bonds. By buying bonds from the market, the RBI injected liquidity into the system, enabling banks to increase their lending capacity to businesses and consumers. This move was aimed at encouraging investment and consumption, which were both critical to reigniting economic growth.

As a result of these OMO purchases, bond yields in India started to fall, which made it cheaper for the government and corporations to borrow funds. Lower bond yields were particularly beneficial for sectors such as infrastructure and real estate, which rely heavily on long-term borrowing. However, the drop in yields also posed a challenge for institutional investors like insurance companies and pension funds, which typically rely on higher bond yields to meet their investment return targets.

Additionally, the RBI's bond-buying program helped stabilize the financial markets during a time of global economic uncertainty. Concerns over the US-China trade war and geopolitical tensions in the Middle East had caused volatility in global financial markets, including India's. By conducting OMOs, the RBI provided a buffer against this external volatility, ensuring that domestic liquidity conditions remained stable.

The RBI's OMO actions also played a key role in managing the fiscal deficit, as the government was able to borrow at lower interest rates to finance its expenditures. However, this large-scale bond purchasing raised concerns about fiscal discipline, as it indirectly supported increased government borrowing, which could lead to long-term challenges if fiscal deficits were not properly managed.

Ultimately, the RBI's OMOs in 2019 succeeded in injecting liquidity, lowering bond yields, and supporting the broader economy during a period of economic slowdown. These measures helped maintain financial stability and ensured that credit was available to key sectors of the economy at a time when growth was faltering.

Questions Based on the Case:

    i.   How did the RBI's open market operations (OMOs) in 2019 affect the Indian bond market and the overall interest rate environment?

    ii.   What were the benefits and challenges associated with the RBI's large-scale bond purchases for both the government and institutional investors?

    iii.   How did the RBI's OMO actions help manage external economic uncertainties, such as the US-China trade war, during this period?

Case Study 3.4: RBI's Open Market Operations to Manage Inflation and Liquidity (2016 Demonetization)

In November 2016, the Government of India announced the demonetization of ₹500 and ₹1000 currency notes, a move aimed at curbing black money, counterfeit currency, and promoting digital payments. This unexpected decision led to an immediate liquidity surplus in the banking system as people rushed to deposit old currency notes in banks. While the demonetization policy had social and economic implications, it also created a challenging situation for the Reserve Bank of India (RBI) in managing the sudden excess liquidity in the financial system. To deal with this, the RBI heavily relied on Open Market Operations (OMOs).

Post-demonetization, the RBI faced a liquidity glut in the banking system as nearly ₹15.44 lakh crore worth of demonetized currency returned to banks. The sudden increase in bank deposits resulted in an excess supply of funds, which had the potential to disrupt the economy by fuelling inflation if not properly managed. To absorb this surplus liquidity and prevent overheating in the economy, the RBI quickly initiated OMOs, particularly focusing on the sale of government securities.

Through these OMOs, the RBI sold a significant amount of government bonds to the banks, thereby mopping up the excess liquidity. This strategy was essential in maintaining a balance between the sudden influx of funds and ensuring that inflation did not spiral out of control. The RBI also introduced other measures, such as the Incremental Cash Reserve Ratio (ICRR), which mandated banks to maintain a higher portion of their deposits as reserves. These actions further tightened liquidity, preventing the economy from being flooded with excessive cash.

While the OMOs helped stabilize the banking system, the period following demonetization was marked by lower interest rates as banks, flush with liquidity, were more inclined to lend at lower rates. This helped in stimulating consumption and investment in the economy. However, the RBI had to remain vigilant to ensure that inflationary pressures, particularly in sectors like real estate and consumer goods, were kept in check.

The RBI's timely intervention through OMOs helped prevent a liquidity-driven inflation surge post-demonetization and ensured that the banking system remained stable during a period of unprecedented cash inflows. The open market operations, along with other monetary tools, enabled the RBI to manage the immediate liquidity crisis effectively while gradually restoring normalcy in the financial markets.

Questions Based on the Case:

i. How did the RBI's open market operations (OMOs) help manage the excess liquidity in the banking system following the 2016 demonetization?

ii. What role did the sale of government securities play in controlling potential inflationary pressures during this period?

iii. How did demonetization and the subsequent OMOs impact interest rates and lending patterns in India's banking sector?

Case Study 3.5: RBI's Use of Open Market Operations to Stabilize the Rupee (2013 Currency Crisis)

In 2013, India faced a major currency crisis when the Indian rupee experienced significant depreciation, largely due to global factors like the tapering of the US Federal Reserve's quantitative easing program. This led to a large outflow of foreign capital from emerging markets, including India. As the demand for US dollars surged, the Indian rupee hit record lows against the dollar, falling from around ₹54 per US dollar in May 2013 to ₹68.85 per US dollar by August 2013. This depreciation created significant challenges for the Indian economy, including increased inflation, higher import costs, and a growing current account deficit.

To address this crisis, the Reserve Bank of India (RBI) stepped in with several measures, one of the most significant being Open Market Operations (OMOs) aimed at stabilizing the rupee and controlling inflation. The RBI's strategy involved the sale of government securities in the domestic market to absorb liquidity. By conducting OMOs, the RBI sought to tighten liquidity in the banking system, thereby making it more difficult for speculative forces to take advantage of the currency volatility.

Additionally, the RBI worked to increase foreign exchange reserves by opening a special dollar swap window for oil marketing companies. This reduced their demand for dollars in the open market, thereby easing pressure on the rupee. The RBI also raised interest rates through repo rate hikes to make the rupee more attractive to foreign investors, helping to stem the outflow of capital.

The sale of government securities through OMOs was particularly important in curbing the inflationary effects of a weak currency. By selling bonds and absorbing excess liquidity, the RBI managed to keep inflation under control while supporting the rupee. The OMO operations were complemented by a slew of other monetary policy measures, such as increasing short-term interest rates and providing liquidity to banks through term repos, to ensure that the rupee remained stable while the economy dealt with external shocks.

Despite these challenges, the RBI's decisive actions, particularly through OMOs and foreign exchange interventions, helped restore investor confidence in the Indian economy. The rupee eventually stabilized, and by the end of 2013, the currency appreciated to around ₹61 per US dollar, demonstrating the effectiveness of the RBI's intervention in the open market to manage liquidity and support the currency.

Questions Based on the Case:

i.   How did the Reserve Bank of India use open market operations (OMOs) to stabilize the Indian rupee during the 2013 currency crisis?
ii. What role did the sale of government securities play in curbing inflationary pressures caused by the rupee's depreciation?
iii. How did the RBI's combination of OMOs and foreign exchange interventions help restore investor confidence in the Indian economy during this period?

CREDIT POLICY

Learning Objectives:

- *Understand what credit policy is and how it helps regulate the flow of credit in the economy.*
- *Learn about the practices and instruments the Reserve Bank of India (RBI) uses under its credit policy to control lending and borrowing in the country.*
- *Explore the difference between credit policy and monetary policy, and how they work together to maintain economic stability.*
- *Understand the concepts of expansionary credit policy (which increases lending) and contractionary credit policy (which reduces lending), and when they are used.*
- *Learn about the theories behind credit policy and how they influence the RBI's decisions on credit regulation.*
- *Recognize the impact of credit policy on businesses, banks, and the overall economy.*

Prof. A. Narasimha Rao
K T S S Satyanarayana

CREDIT POLICY

Credit policy refers to the guidelines, procedures, and standards that a company or financial institution uses to determine whether to grant credit to customers and under what terms.

This can include factors such as credit history, income, collateral, and payment history. The credit policy helps to manage credit risk, set credit limits, and establish payment terms and conditions.

The goal of a credit policy is to minimize the risk of default while maximizing the opportunity to generate revenue through lending.

A. CREDIT POLICY OF RBI

The Reserve Bank of India (RBI) is the central bank of India and is responsible for implementing monetary policy in the country. As part of its monetary policy, the RBI sets the credit policy, which refers to the guidelines, procedures, and standards it uses to regulate and influence the flow of credit in the Indian economy.

The RBI's credit policy includes various tools and measures to control the money supply, manage interest rates, and regulate the flow of credit to different sectors of the economy. These measures can include changes in the repo rate, cash reserve ratio (CRR), statutory liquidity ratio (SLR), and open market operations. The RBI also implements regulations and guidelines to ensure that the banking sector operates in a safe, sound, and stable manner, and to protect the interests of depositors.

The RBI's credit policy is designed to maintain price stability, promote financial stability, and support economic growth. The central bank periodically reviews and updates its credit policy based on the current economic conditions and the outlook for the future. The key aspects of credit policy in India are as follows:

1. Monetary policy framework:

The Reserve Bank of India (RBI) sets the monetary policy framework for the country, which includes setting the benchmark interest rates and regulating the money supply to ensure price stability.

2. Lending rates:

The RBI sets guidelines for the lending rates of commercial banks, which affects the cost of borrowing for consumers and businesses. The RBI also monitors the credit growth of commercial banks to ensure that lending is done in a responsible manner.

3. Priority sector lending:

The RBI mandates that a certain percentage of the total lending of commercial banks should be directed towards priority sectors such as agriculture, micro, small and medium enterprises (MSMEs), and housing for the economically weaker sections (EWS) and low-income groups (LIG).

4. Credit quality:

The RBI monitors the quality of credit provided by commercial banks, and takes measures to ensure that the banks maintain adequate provisioning for bad loans and manage credit risks.

5. Financial inclusion:

The RBI promotes financial inclusion by providing guidelines for banks to open branches in unbanked areas, and by promoting the use of digital financial services to reach the underserved population.

6. Regulatory framework:

The RBI regulates non-banking financial companies (NBFCs) and other financial institutions to ensure financial stability, and has the authority to take corrective actions against institutions that do not comply with the regulations.

7. International trade and capital flows:

The RBI regulates the flow of capital in and out of the country, and takes measures to maintain a stable balance of payments position.

Overall, the credit policy in India is designed to promote inclusive economic growth while ensuring financial stability. The RBI plays a crucial role in setting the policy framework and regulating the financial system to achieve these objectives.

B. PRACTICES OF CREDIT POLICY

Credit policy practices refer to the specific actions and measures that are taken by credit providers (such as banks, financial institutions, and central banks) to implement their credit policies.

These practices can vary depending on the goals and objectives of the credit policy, as well as the specific circumstances and conditions of the economy.

Here are some common practices of credit policy:

1. Setting interest rates:

This refers to adjusting the cost of borrowing, which can impact the demand for credit and the flow of funds in the economy.

2. Regulating the money supply:

This refers to controlling the amount of money in circulation, which can impact the availability of credit and the overall level of economic activity.

3. Lending standards and criteria:

This refers to establishing the criteria that must be met by borrowers in order to be approved for credit. This can include factors such as credit history, income, collateral, and payment history.

4. Managing credit risk:

This refers to the measures taken to minimize the risk of default by borrowers and to ensure that the credit provider is protected.

5. Establishing credit limits:

This refers to setting maximum levels of credit that can be extended to individual borrowers or to specific sectors of the economy.

6. Monitoring and reporting:

This refers to regular monitoring of credit trends and market conditions and reporting the results to relevant authorities and stakeholders.

7. Supervision and regulation:

This refers to the oversight and enforcement of credit policies by government agencies and other regulatory bodies.

These practices are designed to help credit providers achieve their goals and objectives as outlined in their credit policy. The specific practices of credit policy can be adjusted and changed over time based on the evolving economic conditions and circumstances.

C. PRACTICES FOLLOWED BY RBI UNDER CREDIT POLICY

The Reserve Bank of India (RBI) implements its credit policy using a variety of tools and measures to regulate the flow of credit in the Indian economy. Here are some common practices followed by the RBI under its credit policy:

1. Setting interest rates:

The RBI sets the repo rate, which is the rate at which commercial banks can borrow money from the central bank. The repo rate is used as a benchmark for determining interest rates in the economy.

2. Regulating the money supply:

The RBI uses the cash reserve ratio (CRR) and the statutory liquidity ratio (SLR) to regulate the money supply in the economy. The CRR is the minimum portion of deposits that commercial banks must hold with the RBI, while the SLR is the minimum portion of deposits that banks must hold in the form of liquid assets.

3. Monitoring and reporting:

The RBI regularly monitors credit and monetary trends in the economy and publishes reports on its monetary policy and credit policy. These reports provide insights into the current state of the economy and the outlook for the future.

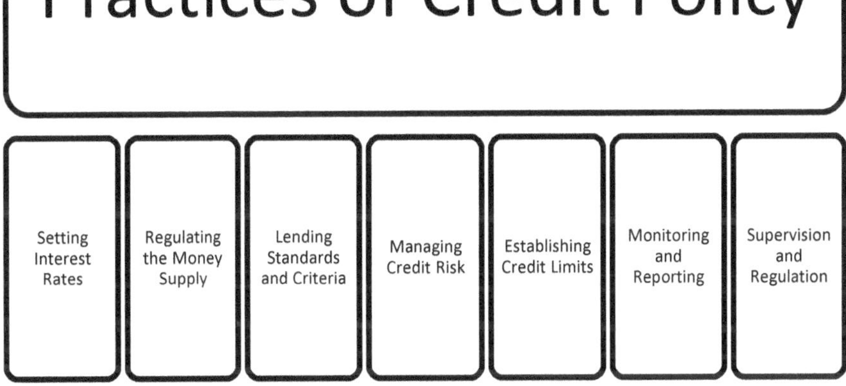

Exhibit 4.1: Practices of Credit Policy

4. Supervision and regulation:

The RBI supervises and regulates the banking sector to ensure that it operates in a safe, sound, and stable manner. This includes implementing regulations and guidelines for banks, conducting regular inspections and audits, and enforcing penalties for non-compliance.

5. Open market operations:

The RBI conducts open market operations, which involve buying and selling government securities, to regulate the money supply in the economy. This can be used to influence interest rates and credit availability.

6. Promoting financial stability:

The RBI implements measures to promote financial stability and protect the interests of depositors. This can include providing liquidity support to banks, supervising and regulating the non-banking financial sector, and taking action against financial institutions that engage in unethical or illegal practices.

These practices are designed to help the RBI achieve its goals of maintaining price stability, promoting financial stability, and supporting economic growth. The specific practices of credit policy can be adjusted and changed over time based on the evolving economic conditions and circumstances.

D. INSTRUMENTS UTILIZED BY RBI UNDER CREDIT POLICY

The Reserve Bank of India (RBI) uses various instruments to implement its credit policy and regulate the flow of credit in the Indian economy.

Here are some of the key instruments utilized by the RBI:

1. Repo Rate:

The repo rate is the rate at which commercial banks can borrow money from the RBI for short periods. By adjusting the repo rate, the RBI can influence the cost of borrowing and the availability of credit in the economy.

2. Reverse Repo Rate:

The reverse repo rate is the rate at which the RBI borrows money from commercial banks for short periods. By adjusting the reverse repo rate, the RBI can influence the returns that banks earn on their excess reserves, and thus influence the overall availability of credit in the economy.

3. Cash Reserve Ratio (CRR):

The CRR is the minimum portion of deposits that commercial banks must hold with the RBI. By adjusting the CRR, the RBI can influence the amount of funds that are available to banks for lending, and thus influence the availability of credit in the economy.

4. Statutory Liquidity Ratio (SLR):

The SLR is the minimum portion of deposits that banks must hold in the form of liquid assets. By adjusting the SLR, the RBI can influence the amount of funds that are available to banks for lending, and thus influence the availability of credit in the economy.

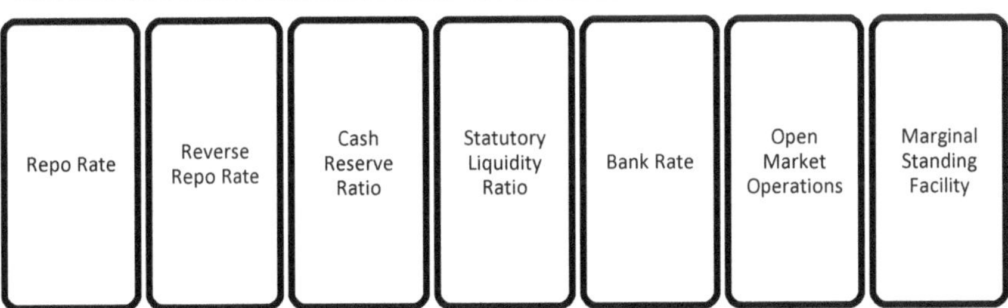

Exhibit 4.2: Instruments Utilized by RBI under Credit Policy

5. Bank Rate:

The bank rate is the rate at which the RBI lends money to commercial banks for longer periods. By adjusting the bank rate, the RBI can influence the cost of borrowing for banks, and thus influence the cost of credit for borrowers.

6. Open Market Operations (OMOs):

The RBI uses OMOs to buy and sell government securities, which can influence the money supply and interest rates in the economy.

7. Marginal Standing Facility (MSF):

The MSF is a borrowing facility for banks, which allows them to borrow funds from the RBI overnight at a higher interest rate. By adjusting the MSF rate, the RBI can influence the cost of borrowing for banks, and thus influence the availability of credit in the economy.

These instruments are used by the RBI in various combinations and with varying intensities to achieve its goals of maintaining price stability, promoting financial stability, and supporting economic growth. The specific instruments used can be adjusted and changed over time based on the evolving economic conditions and circumstances.

E. CREDIT POLICY VS MONETARY POLICY

Credit policy and monetary policy are both tools used by central banks, such as the Reserve Bank of India (RBI), to regulate the economy. However, there are some key differences between these two policies:

Description	Monetary policy	Credit policy
Objectives	The objective of monetary policy is to regulate the money supply, interest rates, and inflation in the	Credit policy, on the other hand, focuses on regulating the flow of credit in the economy.

	economy.	
Scope	Monetary policy is a broader concept that encompasses various tools, such as interest rate adjustments, reserve requirements, and open market operations	It is a narrower concept that focuses specifically on regulating the availability and cost of credit in the economy.
Implementation	Monetary policy is typically implemented through the central bank's interest rate adjustments and other monetary tools.	It is implemented through various measures, such as setting reserve requirements, adjusting credit limits, and providing refinancing facilities.
Impact	Monetary policy has a broader impact on the economy, affecting inflation, employment, and economic growth.	It has a more direct impact on the financial sector, affecting the availability and cost of credit for borrowers.

Exhibit 4.3: Difference Between Monetary Policy and Credit Policy

In summary, while both credit policy and monetary policy are tools used by central banks to regulate the economy, they differ in their objectives, scope, implementation, and impact.

F. EXPANSIONARY CREDIT POLICY & CONTRACTIONARY CREDIT POLICY

Expansionary credit policy and contractionary credit policy are two types of credit policies that central banks use to manage the economy.

1. Expansionary Credit Policy:

This policy is used to stimulate economic growth and increase the money supply. The central bank may implement this policy by lowering interest rates, reducing reserve requirements for banks, or buying government securities in the open market.

By making credit more readily available and cheaper, businesses and individuals are encouraged to borrow more, invest more, and spend more, which can lead to increased economic activity and job creation.

Expansionary policies can stimulate economic growth but may lead to inflation if not managed properly.

2. Contractionary Credit Policy:

This policy is used to slow down inflation and reduce economic growth. The central bank may implement this policy by raising interest rates, increasing reserve requirements for banks, or selling government securities in the open market.

By making credit less available and more expensive, businesses and individuals are discouraged from borrowing, investing, and spending, which can lead to a decrease in economic activity and job creation.

Contractionary policies can help control inflation but may lead to a recession if implemented too aggressively.

Both expansionary and contractionary credit policies have their advantages and disadvantages. Central banks must carefully balance these policies to achieve their macroeconomic objectives.

G. THEORIES OF CREDIT POLICY:

There are several theories of credit policy that help us understand the role of credit in the economy and the mechanisms through which credit policy can be used to achieve specific objectives.

Here are some of the key theories of credit policy:

1. Quantitative Theory of Credit

The Quantity Theory of Credit is a theory of credit policy that suggests that the total volume of credit in an economy is a key determinant of economic growth and stability. According to this theory, an increase in the volume of credit can lead to an increase in economic activity, while a decrease in credit can lead to a decrease in economic activity.

Theories of Credit Policy

Quantitative Theory of Credit	Keynesian Theory of Credit	Structuralist Theory of Credit	Monetarist Theory of Credit	Financial Accelerator Theory

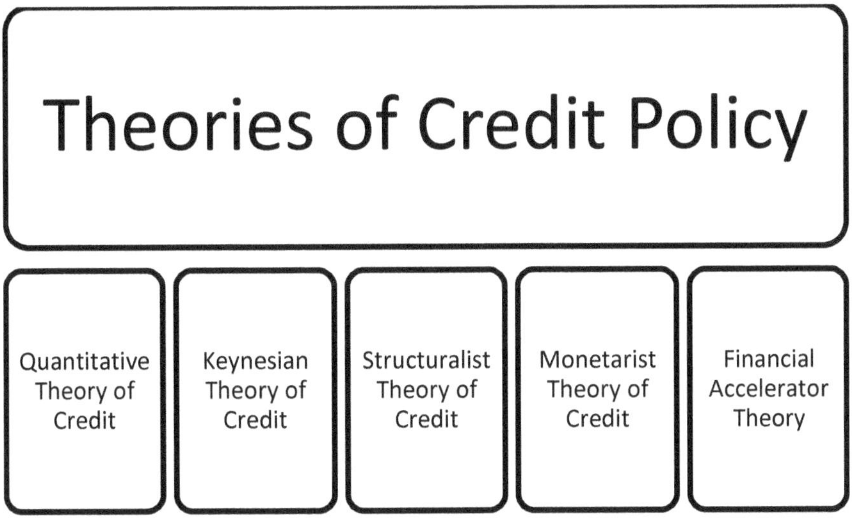

Exhibit 4.4: Theories of Credit Policy

The Quantity Theory of Credit is based on the Quantity Theory of Money, which is a theory of monetary economics that suggests that the total supply of money in an economy is a key determinant of inflation. The Quantity Theory of Credit extends this idea to credit, suggesting that the total volume of credit in an economy is a key determinant of economic activity.

The Quantity Theory of Credit suggests that there is a direct relationship between the volume of credit in the economy and the level of economic activity. As the volume of credit increases, there is more money available for investment, consumption, and other economic activities. This, in turn, leads to increased economic activity, as businesses expand, employment increases, and consumer spending rises.

However, the Quantity Theory of Credit also suggests that there is a limit to the amount of credit that can be extended without causing economic instability. If the volume of credit increases too rapidly, it can lead to inflation, asset bubbles, and financial instability. Therefore, the central bank must carefully regulate the volume of credit in the economy to promote economic growth and stability.

To regulate the volume of credit, the central bank can use a variety of tools, including setting interest rates, adjusting reserve requirements, and providing refinancing facilities. By using these tools, the central bank can influence the availability and cost of credit in the economy, and promote economic growth and stability.

Overall, the Quantity Theory of Credit is an important theory of credit policy that highlights the role of credit in the economy and the mechanisms through which credit policy can be used to promote economic growth and stability. By regulating the volume of credit in the economy, the central bank can help ensure that credit is available to support economic activity, while also maintaining financial stability.

2. Keynesian Theory of Credit:

The Keynesian Theory of Credit is a theory of credit policy that suggests that credit plays a crucial role in determining the level of aggregate demand in the economy. According to this theory, credit policy can be used to stimulate demand by making credit more available and affordable to consumers and businesses. This, in turn, can lead to increased economic activity and employment.

The Keynesian Theory of Credit is based on the ideas of John Maynard Keynes, a prominent economist of the 20th century. Keynes argued that in times of economic recession, the private sector may not be able to generate enough demand to keep the economy at full employment. In this situation, he suggested that the government should step in and increase its own spending to stimulate demand and promote economic growth.

However, Keynes also recognized that government spending alone may not be sufficient to stimulate demand in the economy. He suggested that credit policy could be used to complement fiscal policy by making credit more available and affordable to consumers and businesses. By lowering interest rates and making credit more accessible, the central bank can encourage borrowing and investment, which can lead to increased economic activity and employment.

The Keynesian Theory of Credit also emphasizes the importance of the credit multiplier effect. This effect suggests that an increase in the supply of credit can lead to a much larger increase in economic activity, as the funds that are borrowed are spent and re-spent multiple times throughout the economy. This means that even small changes in credit availability can have a significant impact on economic activity.

To implement the Keynesian Theory of Credit, the central bank can use a variety of tools, including setting interest rates, adjusting reserve requirements, and providing refinancing facilities. By using these tools, the central bank can influence the availability and cost of credit in the economy, and promote economic growth and stability.

Overall, the Keynesian Theory of Credit is an important theory of credit policy that emphasizes the role of credit in promoting economic growth and stability. By making credit more accessible and affordable, the central bank can stimulate demand and promote economic activity, while also helping to maintain financial stability.

3. Structuralist Theory of Credit

The Structuralist Theory of Credit is a theory of credit policy that suggests that credit can be used to support economic development and structural transformation. According to this theory, credit policy can be used to address structural constraints in the economy, such as limited access to finance and inadequate infrastructure, and promote long-term economic growth.

The Structuralist Theory of Credit is based on the ideas of structuralism, a school of thought in economics that emphasizes the importance of economic structures and institutions in determining economic outcomes. Structuralists argue that economic development requires changes in the underlying economic structures and institutions of a society, such as the development of infrastructure, institutions for property rights and contract enforcement, and education and training systems.

According to the Structuralist Theory of Credit, credit policy can play a critical role in promoting structural transformation by providing financing for investment in infrastructure, human capital, and productive capacity. This, in turn, can lead to increased productivity, employment, and long-term economic growth.

However, the Structuralist Theory of Credit also recognizes that credit policy must be designed in a way that supports the development of the economy and does not create excessive debt burdens or financial instability. This requires careful consideration of the types of projects and investments that are financed with credit, as well as the terms and conditions of credit provision.

To implement the Structuralist Theory of Credit, the central bank can use a variety of tools, including setting interest rates, providing credit guarantees and subsidies, and developing specialized financial institutions for specific sectors of the economy. By using these tools, the central bank can influence the direction and focus of credit provision, and promote long-term economic growth and structural transformation.

Overall, the Structuralist Theory of Credit is an important theory of credit policy that emphasizes the role of credit in supporting long-term economic growth and structural transformation. By providing financing for investment in infrastructure, human capital, and productive capacity, credit policy can help address structural constraints in the economy and promote economic development.

4. Monetarist Theory of Credit

The Monetarist Theory of Credit is a theory of credit policy that emphasizes the importance of controlling the money supply to achieve stable economic growth and low inflation. According to this theory, credit policy should focus on controlling the supply of money and credit in the economy, rather than manipulating interest rates or providing targeted financing.

The Monetarist Theory of Credit is based on the ideas of Milton Friedman, a prominent economist of the 20th century. Friedman argued that changes in the money supply are the primary driver of changes in aggregate demand and economic activity. He suggested that central banks should focus on controlling the money supply to achieve long-term economic stability.

According to the Monetarist Theory of Credit, an increase in the money supply can lead to inflation and a decrease in the value of money, while a decrease in the money supply can lead to deflation and economic recession. Therefore, the central bank should aim to keep the money supply growing at a steady rate to promote stable economic growth and low inflation.

To implement the Monetarist Theory of Credit, the central bank can use a variety of tools, including open market operations, reserve requirements, and discount rates. By using these tools, the central bank can control the supply of money and credit in the economy, and influence aggregate demand and economic activity.

The Monetarist Theory of Credit also emphasizes the importance of the quantity theory of money. This theory suggests that the level of prices in the economy is directly proportional to the money supply, assuming that the velocity of money (the rate at which money changes hands) and the level of output remain constant. This means that controlling the money supply is key to controlling inflation and achieving economic stability.

Overall, the Monetarist Theory of Credit is an important theory of credit policy that emphasizes the importance of controlling the money supply to achieve stable economic growth and low inflation. By focusing on controlling the supply of money and credit in the economy, the central bank can promote economic stability and ensure long-term economic growth.

5. Financial Accelerator Theory

The Financial Accelerator Theory is a theory that explains how changes in financial conditions can affect the real economy through credit markets. According to this theory, changes in financial conditions, such as interest rates, asset prices, and credit availability, can have a magnified impact on the real economy, leading to amplification of economic cycles.

The Financial Accelerator Theory is based on the idea that changes in financial conditions can affect the balance sheets of households and firms, which in turn can affect their spending and investment decisions. For example, if interest rates rise, households and firms may reduce their borrowing and investment, leading to a slowdown in economic activity. Conversely, if interest rates fall, households and firms may increase their borrowing and investment, leading to an acceleration of economic activity.

The Financial Accelerator Theory also suggests that changes in financial conditions can have a magnified impact on the real economy through credit markets. When financial conditions tighten, credit markets may become less accessible, leading to a reduction in borrowing and investment by households and firms. This reduction in borrowing and investment can, in turn, lead to a decline in economic activity. Conversely, when financial conditions ease, credit markets may become more accessible, leading to an increase in borrowing and investment by households and firms, which can lead to an acceleration of economic activity.

To implement the Financial Accelerator Theory, the central bank can use a variety of tools, including setting interest rates, providing liquidity to financial markets, and regulating financial institutions. By using these tools, the central bank can influence financial conditions and promote economic stability.

Overall, the Financial Accelerator Theory is an important theory of credit policy that emphasizes the role of financial conditions in affecting the real economy through credit markets. By understanding the amplification effects of changes in financial conditions, the central bank can use credit policy to promote economic stability and prevent economic cycles from becoming too severe.

In summary, the different theories of credit policy provide different perspectives on the role of credit in the economy and the mechanisms through which credit policy can be used to achieve specific objectives. Understanding these theories can help policymakers develop effective credit policies that promote economic growth and stability.

CHAPTER SUMMARY

CREDIT POLICY

The chapter on Credit Policy delves into the Reserve Bank of India's (RBI) framework for regulating the availability and cost of credit in the Indian economy. It begins with an introduction to the Credit Policy of RBI, explaining its vital role in controlling inflation, promoting economic growth, and maintaining financial stability by influencing the lending behavior of banks and financial institutions.

The chapter outlines the practices followed by the RBI under credit policy, which include the regulation of interest rates, lending limits, and the quality of credit extended by banks. By setting these parameters, the RBI ensures that credit is allocated efficiently to support productive sectors of the economy while safeguarding against excessive risk-taking by banks.

The instruments utilized by the RBI under credit policy are discussed, including the Cash Reserve Ratio (CRR), Statutory Liquidity Ratio (SLR), and bank rate adjustments. These instruments enable the RBI to either expand or contract the availability of credit, depending on the current economic conditions.

A significant section of the chapter contrasts Credit Policy vs. Monetary Policy, explaining how credit policy focuses more specifically on influencing the flow of credit and investment, while monetary policy deals with broader control over money supply and interest rates. Both policies, however, work in tandem to maintain macroeconomic balance.

The chapter also covers the concepts of expansionary credit policy and contractionary credit policy. Expansionary credit policy is used during periods of economic slowdown to boost lending and stimulate economic activity, whereas contractionary credit policy is employed to cool down an overheated economy by tightening credit conditions.

Furthermore, the chapter explores theories of credit policy, which provide a theoretical basis for the tools and strategies used by central banks worldwide, including India, to regulate credit markets.

In conclusion, this chapter emphasizes the importance of the RBI's credit policy in steering the Indian economy toward sustainable growth. By controlling the availability and cost of credit through various instruments, the RBI ensures financial stability, supports productive economic activities, and manages inflationary pressures. The coordination between credit policy and monetary policy is vital in maintaining the overall balance between liquidity and economic growth.

CASE STUDIES

Case Study 4.1: RBI's Credit Policy and Its Role in Supporting MSMEs Post-COVID-19 (2020-2021)

The COVID-19 pandemic had a devastating impact on economies worldwide, and India's MSME (Micro, Small, and Medium Enterprises) sector was particularly affected due to its reliance on short-term credit and demand-sensitive markets. In response to the financial challenges faced by this sector, the Reserve Bank of India (RBI) implemented a series of credit policy interventions aimed at providing liquidity and improving access to credit for MSMEs.

One of the key measures introduced by the RBI was the expansion of the Targeted Long-Term Repo Operations (TLTROs). Under this policy, banks were given long-term liquidity at low-interest rates, specifically to provide credit to sectors in need, including MSMEs. This ensured that liquidity reached businesses most in need of financing during the pandemic. Additionally, the RBI relaxed several regulatory norms, including moratoriums on loan repayments, and extended deadlines for banks to restructure existing loans of MSMEs under the Restructuring Framework 2.0. This restructuring framework allowed banks to give borrowers more time to repay loans without classifying them as non-performing assets (NPAs).

Moreover, the RBI's Emergency Credit Line Guarantee Scheme (ECLGS) was expanded, offering 100% guarantee coverage for additional credit to eligible MSMEs. By enhancing credit flow through these targeted schemes, the RBI aimed to reduce the financial burden on MSMEs and allow them to survive during a period of economic uncertainty and reduced demand.

The RBI's efforts were supported by further policy actions, including lowering the repo rate and providing special liquidity facilities to non-banking financial companies (NBFCs), which play a crucial role in financing MSMEs. By maintaining an accommodative stance in its credit policy, the RBI was able to inject liquidity into the financial system and encourage lending to this critical sector, which employs millions of people and is key to the Indian economy's recovery.

These credit policies played a crucial role in keeping MSMEs afloat during the challenging economic circumstances brought on by the pandemic. They helped ensure that MSMEs could access much-needed credit at affordable rates and gave them the breathing room needed to restructure existing debts and continue their operations despite the economic downturn.

Questions Based on the Case:

i. How did the RBI's credit policy interventions support MSMEs during the COVID-19 pandemic?

ii. What role did the Targeted Long-Term Repo Operations (TLTROs) and the Emergency Credit Line Guarantee Scheme (ECLGS) play in improving access to credit for MSMEs?

iii. How did the RBI's credit policies, including loan restructuring and liquidity measures, help mitigate the financial impact of the pandemic on the MSME sector?

Case Study 4.2: RBI's Credit Policy and the Revival of the Indian Housing Sector (2021)

In the aftermath of the COVID-19 pandemic, the housing sector in India experienced a significant slowdown due to disruptions in construction, a decline in demand, and limited financing options. Recognizing the critical role of the real estate sector in generating employment and driving economic growth, the Reserve Bank of India (RBI) introduced several credit policy measures aimed at reviving the housing sector and stimulating demand.

One of the key interventions was the reduction in repo rates, which the RBI consistently lowered in 2020 and 2021 to historic lows, eventually reaching 4%. This reduction had a direct impact on the interest rates for home loans, making borrowing cheaper for homebuyers. With lower interest rates, banks and housing finance companies (HFCs) were able to offer home loans at competitive rates, which incentivized potential buyers to invest in real estate. The credit policy not only boosted demand for housing but also spurred construction activity, aiding the recovery of the sector.

Another significant credit policy measure was the extension of the Co-Lending Model (CLM), where banks and non-banking financial companies (NBFCs) worked together to provide loans, especially in the priority sectors like affordable housing. Under this model, NBFCs would originate loans, while banks would take a majority share of the funding, allowing for greater access to credit at lower rates for homebuyers. This collaborative approach expanded credit access and supported housing finance, especially for affordable housing projects.

The RBI also increased the loan-to-value (LTV) ratio for housing loans, allowing banks to lend a higher percentage of the property value, which further encouraged homeownership. Additionally, to ensure liquidity in the sector, the RBI provided special liquidity facilities to NBFCs and HFCs, which play a crucial role in financing the real estate sector. This liquidity injection helped these institutions meet the rising demand for housing loans and manage their existing credit portfolios.

Moreover, the RBI's relaxation of asset classification norms gave relief to housing finance companies and borrowers who were struggling to meet repayment obligations due to pandemic-related disruptions. These measures provided a buffer to both lenders and borrowers, allowing more time for recovery without the immediate risk of loans turning into non-performing assets (NPAs).

Overall, the RBI's credit policies, through a combination of rate cuts, liquidity support, and regulatory relaxations, played a pivotal role in reviving the housing sector in India. These interventions not only helped boost homebuyer confidence but also provided much-needed support to the construction industry, which is a key driver of economic growth and employment in the country.

Questions Based on the Case:

i. How did the RBI's reduction in repo rates impact the housing sector and home loan interest rates in India post-COVID-19?

ii. What was the role of the Co-Lending Model (CLM) in expanding credit access for homebuyers, particularly in the affordable housing segment?

iii. How did the RBI's special liquidity facilities and relaxation of asset classification norms contribute to the revival of the housing finance sector?

Case Study 4.3: The Role of RBI's Credit Policy in Strengthening the Agricultural Sector (2021-2022)

India's agricultural sector is the backbone of its economy, employing a significant portion of the population and contributing heavily to GDP. However, the sector is often constrained by a lack of access to credit, particularly for small and marginal farmers. Recognizing these challenges, the Reserve Bank of India (RBI) implemented several credit policy measures aimed at improving credit flow to agriculture and promoting financial inclusion in rural areas.

One of the key interventions by the RBI was the promotion of Priority Sector Lending (PSL), where banks are mandated to lend a specific percentage of their total credit to sectors deemed as "priority," including agriculture. The RBI revised the PSL guidelines to ensure better credit access for small and marginal farmers, setting sub-targets for these groups to ensure that a greater proportion of loans reached those most in need. This policy shift helped enhance the availability of formal credit for rural farmers, reducing their reliance on informal moneylenders who often charge exorbitant interest rates.

To further boost credit flow to the agricultural sector, the RBI increased the Kisan Credit Card (KCC) coverage. The KCC scheme provides farmers with easy and timely credit for crop production, post-harvest expenses, and other agricultural needs. The RBI, in collaboration with public sector banks and cooperative banks, encouraged wider adoption of the KCC scheme, simplifying the application process and making it easier for farmers to access credit. This allowed millions of farmers to meet their short-term credit needs without falling into debt traps.

In addition to these measures, the RBI supported agricultural credit refinancing through the National Bank for Agriculture and Rural Development (NABARD). By providing liquidity support to banks engaged in agricultural lending, the RBI ensured that financial institutions had enough resources to meet the growing credit demand from the agricultural sector. This liquidity support was essential during the post-COVID recovery period, when many rural households faced financial hardships.

The RBI also encouraged digital credit initiatives in rural areas, which aimed at improving access to credit for farmers through digital platforms and fintech solutions. By promoting digital lending solutions, the RBI aimed to reduce the geographical and operational barriers to credit access for rural farmers, increasing financial inclusion in underbanked regions.

Overall, the RBI's credit policies for the agricultural sector played a pivotal role in enhancing access to formal credit, promoting rural financial inclusion, and supporting the recovery of the agricultural economy post-pandemic. These interventions helped ensure that farmers had adequate financial resources to sustain their agricultural activities, improve productivity, and contribute to the overall economic recovery of the country.

Questions Based on the Case:

i. How did the RBI's Priority Sector Lending (PSL) guidelines enhance credit access for small and marginal farmers in India?

ii. What role did the Kisan Credit Card (KCC) scheme play in improving access to formal credit for rural farmers?

iii.   How did the RBI's support for agricultural credit refinancing through NABARD contribute to the recovery of the agricultural sector post-COVID-19?

Case Study 4.4: RBI's Expansionary Credit Policy and MSME Sector Growth (2020-2021)

The Micro, Small, and Medium Enterprises (MSME) sector is a critical component of India's economy, contributing significantly to employment and GDP. However, the MSME sector was one of the hardest hits by the COVID-19 pandemic, facing challenges such as liquidity shortages, decreased demand, and supply chain disruptions. To address these challenges, the Reserve Bank of India (RBI) implemented a series of expansionary credit policy measures aimed at revitalizing the MSME sector and ensuring its survival and recovery.

One of the most impactful interventions was the Emergency Credit Line Guarantee Scheme (ECLGS), which was launched by the government of India in collaboration with the RBI. The scheme provided 100% government-guaranteed loans to MSMEs to help them meet their working capital requirements. The RBI played a crucial role in ensuring that banks provided timely credit to eligible MSMEs under this scheme. This measure helped MSMEs address immediate liquidity shortages, retain their workforce, and continue operations during the economic downturn.

In addition to the ECLGS, the RBI introduced regulatory forbearance measures for the MSME sector. These measures included a moratorium on loan repayments and asset classification relaxations, allowing MSMEs to defer their loan repayments without the risk of loans being classified as non-performing assets (NPAs). This provided breathing room for MSMEs struggling with cash flow issues, allowing them to stabilize their operations during the challenging period.

The RBI also provided liquidity support to Non-Banking Financial Companies (NBFCs), which are key lenders to the MSME sector. By ensuring that NBFCs had adequate liquidity through the Targeted Long-Term Repo Operations (TLTRO), the RBI ensured that NBFCs could continue lending to MSMEs. This was particularly important as NBFCs often cater to the credit needs of smaller businesses that do not have access to formal banking channels.

Furthermore, the RBI's Credit Guarantee Fund Trust for Micro and Small Enterprises (CGTMSE) was strengthened, allowing MSMEs to avail collateral-free loans more easily. By providing guarantees to lenders, this scheme enabled MSMEs to access credit without the need for extensive collateral, which is often a barrier for small businesses.

The expansionary credit policies implemented by the RBI not only helped MSMEs survive the immediate economic shock caused by the pandemic but also laid the groundwork for their recovery and growth. By ensuring that banks, NBFCs, and other financial institutions continued lending to the MSME sector, the RBI's credit policy played a pivotal role in supporting one of the most vital sectors of the Indian economy.

Questions Based on the Case:

i. How did the Emergency Credit Line Guarantee Scheme (ECLGS) help MSMEs address liquidity shortages during the COVID-19 pandemic?

ii. What role did the RBI's regulatory forbearance measures play in supporting MSMEs' financial stability during the economic downturn?

iii. How did the RBI's liquidity support to NBFCs through the Targeted Long-Term Repo Operations (TLTRO) benefit the MSME sector?

FISCAL POLICY

Learning Objectives:

- *Understand what fiscal policy is and how it helps the government manage the economy through spending and taxation.*
- *Learn about the main goals of fiscal policy in India, like promoting economic growth, reducing unemployment, and controlling inflation.*
- *Explore the different types of budgets prepared by the Indian government, including the Union Budget and State Budget, and why they are important for the economy.*
- *Understand the sources of finance for both the central and state governments, and how the government raises money.*
- *Learn about the role of the Finance Commission in India, its functions, and how it helps in the fair distribution of resources between the central and state governments.*
- *Explore how the government tries to strike a balance between inflation and economic growth using both fiscal and monetary policies.*

FISCAL POLICY

Fiscal policy refers to the use of government spending, taxation, and borrowing to influence the economy. The main goal of fiscal policy is to stabilize the economy by promoting economic growth, controlling inflation, and reducing unemployment.

The government can use expansionary fiscal policy to stimulate the economy during a recession by increasing spending and cutting taxes, which can increase demand and encourage businesses to invest and hire more workers. Conversely, contractionary fiscal policy can be used during times of inflation to slow down the economy by decreasing spending and raising taxes, which can reduce demand and encourage people to save more.

Fiscal policy can also be used to address specific economic issues, such as income inequality, by providing social welfare programs or adjusting tax rates for different income brackets. Additionally, the government can use fiscal policy to invest in infrastructure projects, such as highways or public transportation, which can help support long-term economic growth.

A. FISCAL POLICY IN INDIA

Fiscal policy in India is primarily formulated and implemented by the Ministry of Finance and the Reserve Bank of India (RBI). The main objectives of fiscal policy in India are to promote economic growth, reduce poverty, and maintain price stability.

The fiscal policy in India is implemented through various tools such as taxation, government spending, subsidies, and public debt management. Here are some of the key aspects of fiscal policy in India:

1. Taxation:

The government collects revenue through direct and indirect taxes such as income tax, goods and services tax (GST), customs and excise duties. The tax policy in India is focused on promoting growth, reducing inequality, and increasing compliance.

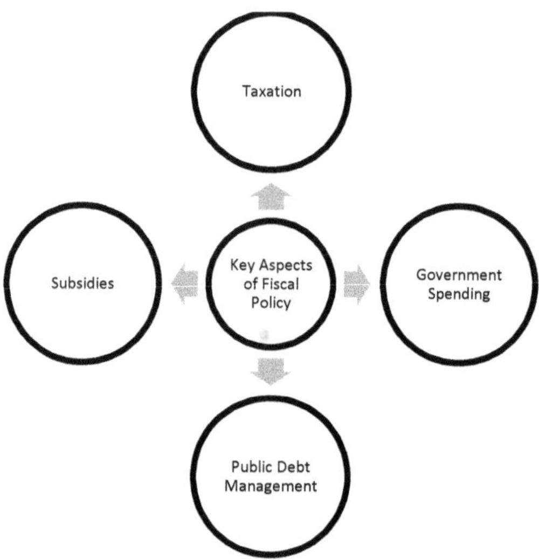

Exhibit 5.1: Key Aspects of Fiscal Policy

2. Government spending:

The government spends on various social welfare programs such as education, healthcare, and subsidies for the poor. The government also invests in infrastructure projects such as roads, highways, and railways to stimulate economic growth.

3. Public debt management:

The government borrows funds through the issuance of government securities, and the RBI manages the public debt. The government tries to maintain a manageable level of debt while ensuring that the borrowing costs are reasonable.

4. Subsidies:

The government provides subsidies to various sectors such as agriculture, food, and energy to support these sectors and ensure that the benefits reach the intended beneficiaries.

Overall, fiscal policy in India is designed to promote economic growth while maintaining stability in the economy. However, like any other country, there are challenges in balancing the competing demands of growth, inflation, and social welfare.

B. FEATURES OF FISCAL POLICY IN INDIA

Here are some of the key features of fiscal policy in India:

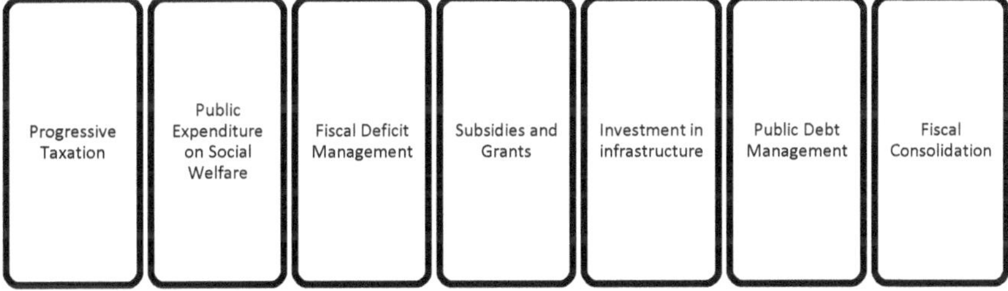

Exhibit 5.2: Features of Fiscal Policy in India

1. Progressive taxation:

The tax system in India is designed to be progressive, which means that the tax burden increases with higher income levels. This helps to reduce income inequality and promote social justice.

2. Public expenditure on social welfare:

The Indian government spends a significant amount of its budget on social welfare programs such as education, healthcare, and rural development. This helps to reduce poverty, improve human development indicators, and promote inclusive growth.

3. Fiscal deficit management:

The Indian government has set targets for managing the fiscal deficit, which is the difference between its total expenditure and revenue. The government aims to keep the fiscal deficit within manageable limits to maintain macroeconomic stability.

4. Subsidies and grants:

The government provides subsidies and grants to various sectors such as agriculture, food, and energy to support these sectors and ensure that the benefits reach the intended beneficiaries.

5. Investment in infrastructure:

The Indian government invests in infrastructure projects such as roads, highways, and railways to stimulate economic growth and create employment opportunities.

6. Public debt management:

The government borrows funds through the issuance of government securities, and the Reserve Bank of India manages the public debt. The government tries to maintain a manageable level of debt while ensuring that the borrowing costs are reasonable.

7. Fiscal consolidation:

The Indian government has been implementing fiscal consolidation measures to reduce its fiscal deficit and improve the overall health of public finances.

Overall, the fiscal policy in India is aimed at promoting economic growth, reducing poverty, and maintaining macroeconomic stability. The government uses a range of fiscal policy tools such as taxation, public expenditure, subsidies, and public debt management to achieve these objectives.

C. OBJECTIVES OF FISCAL POLICY IN INDIA

The primary objectives of fiscal policy in India are to promote economic growth, reduce poverty and income inequality, and maintain price stability. The Indian government uses fiscal policy to achieve these objectives by employing a range of tools such as government spending, taxation, subsidies, and public debt management.

Objectives of Fiscal Policy in India

| Promote Economic Growth | Reduce Proverty and Income Inequality | Maintain Price Stability | Ensure Financial Stability |

Exhibit 5.3: Objectives of Fiscal Policy in India

1. Promote economic growth:

One of the main objectives of fiscal policy in India is to promote economic growth. The government achieves this by investing in infrastructure, providing subsidies, and encouraging private investment. The government also aims to create a conducive business environment that supports entrepreneurship and innovation.

2. Reduce poverty and income inequality:

Another key objective of fiscal policy in India is to reduce poverty and income inequality. The government provides subsidies and social welfare programs, such as the Mahatma Gandhi National Rural Employment Guarantee Act (MGNREGA), to provide employment opportunities and reduce poverty. The tax system is also designed to be progressive, with higher tax rates for higher-income earners, to reduce income inequality.

3. Maintain price stability:

The Indian government aims to maintain price stability by controlling inflation. The government can use fiscal policy tools, such as taxation and public expenditure, to control inflation and stabilize the economy. The Reserve Bank of India (RBI) also plays a key role in maintaining price stability through monetary policy.

4. Ensure financial stability:

Fiscal policy in India aims to ensure financial stability by managing public debt and maintaining a sustainable fiscal deficit. The government aims to keep its borrowing costs at a reasonable level and avoid excessive debt levels, which can compromise macroeconomic stability.

Overall, the main objectives of fiscal policy in India are to promote economic growth, reduce poverty and income inequality, maintain price stability, and ensure financial stability. The Indian government uses a range of fiscal policy tools to achieve these objectives and support sustainable economic development.

D. SOURCES OF FINANCE TO STATE AND CENTRAL GOVERNMENT

The Central and State Governments in India have various sources of finance to fund their expenditures. Some of the major sources of finance for the Central and State Governments are:

1. Tax Revenue:

Tax revenue is the largest source of income for the Central and State Governments. This includes income tax, corporate tax, goods and services tax (GST), excise duty, customs duty, and other taxes.

2. Non-Tax Revenue:

Non-tax revenue includes income from sources other than taxes such as dividends, interest, and profits from public sector enterprises, fees for various services provided by the government, and revenue from the sale of government assets.

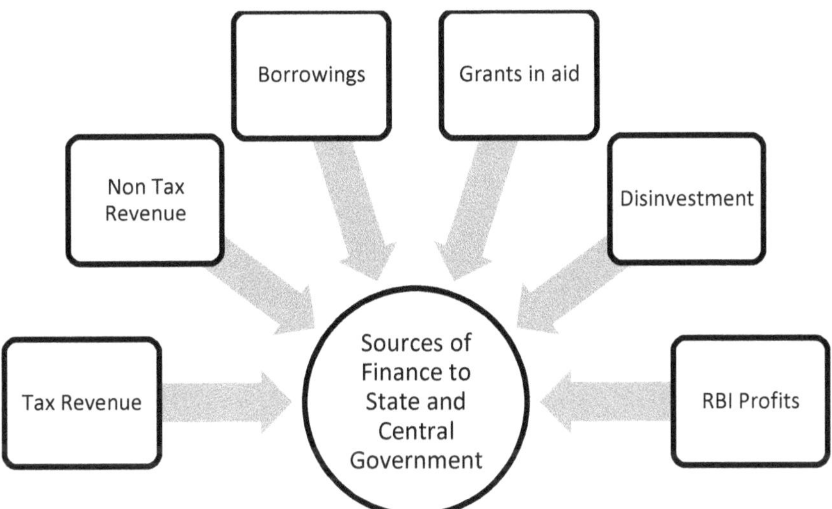

Exhibit 5.4: Sources of Finance to State and Central Government

3. Borrowings:

Both the Central and State Governments borrow from domestic and international markets to finance their expenditures. The government issues bonds and securities to raise funds from the public, banks, and financial institutions.

4. Grants-in-aid:

The Central Government provides grants-in-aid to the State Governments to finance various projects and schemes. These grants are used to fund capital expenditures in areas such as health, education, and infrastructure.

5. Disinvestment:

Disinvestment refers to the sale of government-owned assets such as public sector companies, land, and other assets. The proceeds from disinvestment can be used to fund government expenditures.

6. Reserve Bank of India (RBI) profits:

The RBI pays a dividend to the Central Government from its profits, which provides a significant source of revenue to the Central Government.

Overall, the Central and State Governments in India have multiple sources of finance to fund their expenditures. The mix of revenue sources varies depending on the policies and economic conditions prevailing at the time. The government's fiscal policy aims to maintain a balance between the various sources of revenue and to ensure that there is no excessive reliance on any one source.

E. BUDGET

A budget is a financial plan that outlines an individual's or an organization's expected income and expenses for a specific period. In the case of a government, a budget is a financial plan that outlines the expected revenue and expenditures for the government's operations during a fiscal year, which is usually a period of 12 months.

The budget is a key tool for a government to allocate resources towards its policy priorities and achieve its goals.

The budget process typically involves the following stages:

1. Budget preparation:

The government prepares a draft budget that outlines the expected revenue and expenditure for the upcoming fiscal year. This involves analyzing the current economic situation, setting policy priorities, and estimating the revenue that will be generated through taxes, fees, and other sources.

2. Budget presentation:

The budget is presented to the parliament or legislative body for review and approval. The budget document typically includes a detailed breakdown of the government's revenue and expenditures, including allocation to specific departments, programs, and services.

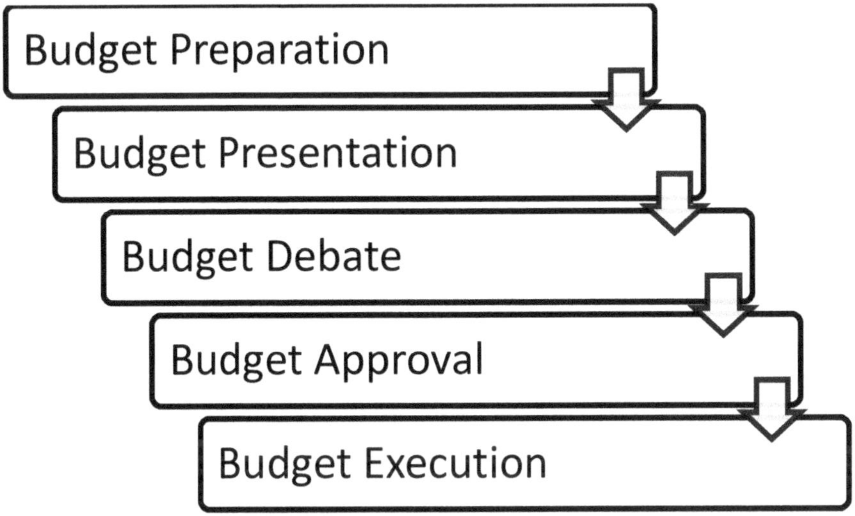

Exhibit 5.5: Stages of Budget Process

3. Budget debate:

The parliament or legislative body debates and scrutinizes the budget to ensure that it is in line with the government's policy priorities and does not compromise macroeconomic stability. The budget can be amended and revised during this stage.

4. Budget approval:

The budget is approved by the parliament or legislative body and becomes law. The government can then implement the budget, allocating resources to different programs and services according to the priorities outlined in the budget document.

5. Budget execution:

The government implements the budget by releasing funds to different departments, programs, and services. The government monitors the execution of the budget to ensure that it is on track and adjusts the budget as needed.

The budget plays a critical role in the functioning of the government and the economy. It helps to ensure that resources are allocated efficiently and effectively, and that the government's policy priorities are achieved.

F. TYPES OF BUDGETS PREPARED BY INDIAN GOVERNMENT

The Indian government prepares several types of budgets to achieve its economic and social objectives.

The main types of budgets prepared by the Indian government are:

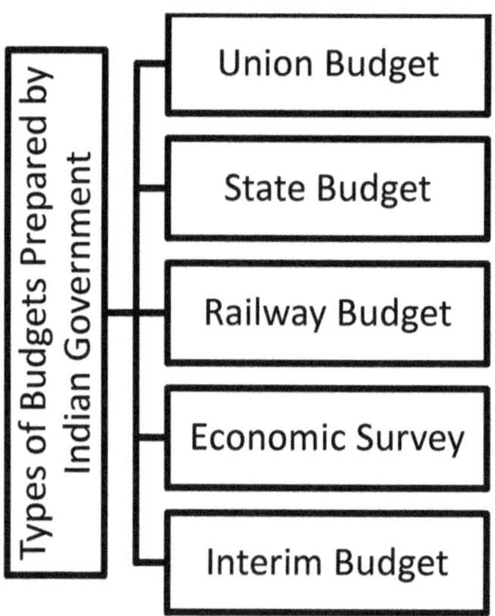

**Exhibit 5.6: Types of Bugets Prepared
by Indian Government**

1. Union Budget:

The Union Budget is the annual financial statement of the central government of India that outlines the government's revenue and expenditure for the upcoming fiscal year. The Union Budget is presented to the parliament by the Finance Minister and includes detailed information on the government's tax policies, expenditure plans, and policy priorities.

2. State Budget:

Each state government in India prepares its own budget to outline its expected revenue and expenditure for the upcoming fiscal year. The State Budget is presented by the respective state Finance Minister and provides information on the state's tax policies, expenditure plans, and policy priorities.

3. Railway Budget:

The Railway Budget is a separate budget presented by the Union Minister for Railways. It outlines the expected revenue and expenditure for the Indian Railways, which is the national railway system in India. The Railway Budget provides information on the railway's investment plans, policy priorities, and performance targets.

4. Economic Survey:

The Economic Survey is a document prepared by the Ministry of Finance that provides an overview of the Indian economy's performance during the previous fiscal year. The Economic Survey includes data on key economic indicators, policy recommendations, and analysis of the current economic situation.

5. Interim Budget:

The Interim Budget is presented by the government in an election year when the full budget cannot be presented due to the upcoming elections. The Interim Budget provides a vote on account, which allows the government to spend money until the new government is formed.

Overall, these different types of budgets play a crucial role in outlining the government's expected revenue and expenditure and help the government achieve its economic and social objectives.

G. IMPORTANCE OF INDIAN GOVERNMENT BUDGETS

The Indian government budgets play a crucial role in the functioning of the economy and the country's overall development.

The following are some of the important reasons why Indian government budgets are important:

1. Allocation of Resources:

The government budget is the primary tool for allocating resources towards the government's policy priorities. The government can use the budget to direct resources towards critical sectors such as health, education, and infrastructure. This ensures that resources are used effectively and efficiently, and that the government can achieve its policy goals.

2. Revenue Generation:

The government budget outlines the expected revenue from various sources, including taxes, fees, and other sources. This helps the government to plan its revenue collection efforts and ensure that it has sufficient resources to fund its programs and services.

3. Fiscal Discipline:

The government budget is an important tool for maintaining fiscal discipline and ensuring macroeconomic stability. The budget sets limits on government spending and ensures that the government does not exceed its borrowing limits. This helps to prevent excessive debt levels and inflation, which can be detrimental to the economy.

4. Transparency and Accountability:

The government budget is a public document that outlines the government's revenue and expenditure plans. This promotes transparency and accountability and allows citizens to scrutinize the government's spending decisions. The budget process also involves parliamentary debates and discussions, which promote public participation and input in the government's spending decisions.

5. Economic Growth:

The government budget plays a critical role in promoting economic growth by investing in infrastructure, providing subsidies and tax incentives, and encouraging private investment. This helps to create jobs, stimulate economic activity, and promote overall economic development.

Overall, the Indian government budgets are important because they help to allocate resources towards the government's policy priorities, generate revenue, maintain fiscal discipline, promote transparency and accountability, and support economic growth and development.

H. UNION BUDGET:

The Union Budget is the annual financial statement of the central government of India. It is presented to the Parliament by the finance minister and outlines the government's revenue and expenditure plans for the upcoming fiscal year, which runs from April 1 to March 31.

The Union Budget is a comprehensive document that provides a detailed overview of the government's policy priorities, revenue generation plans, and expenditure plans. It includes information on tax policies, subsidies, and grants to states, as well as funding for various government schemes and programs.

The Union Budget is divided into two parts: the Revenue Budget and the Capital Budget. The Revenue Budget includes the government's revenue receipts and expenditures on various programs and schemes, while the Capital Budget includes capital receipts and capital expenditures, such as investments in infrastructure and other long-term assets.

The Union Budget is also an important tool for promoting economic growth and development. The government can use the budget to allocate resources towards critical sectors such as health, education, and infrastructure, which can help to create jobs and stimulate economic activity. The budget also includes measures to promote private investment and business growth, such as tax incentives and subsidies.

The Union Budget process in India involves several stages. The government starts preparing the budget several months before the beginning of the fiscal year, and it is presented to the Parliament on the last working day of February. The Parliament then debates and scrutinizes the budget, and it is typically approved in April, before the beginning of the new fiscal year.

Overall, the Union Budget is a crucial document for the Indian government and plays a critical role in allocating resources, promoting economic growth and development, and maintaining macroeconomic stability.

I. COMPONENTS OF UNION BUDGET

The Union Budget of India consists of several components, including:

1. Budget Speech:

This is the Finance Minister's speech delivered in the Parliament that outlines the government's economic policies and priorities for the upcoming fiscal year.

2. Annual Financial Statement:

This statement includes details of the government's revenue and expenditure plans for the upcoming fiscal year. It includes the estimates of receipts and expenditure for the year, as well as the manner in which the funds will be raised and spent.

3. Demand for Grants:

The Demand for Grants is a detailed statement of the proposed expenditure of various ministries and departments for the upcoming fiscal year. It includes estimates of the amounts required for each scheme or program, and the justification for the proposed expenditure.

4. Appropriation Bill:

The Appropriation Bill is introduced in the Parliament after the Budget is passed, and it provides for the withdrawal of funds from the Consolidated Fund of India for meeting the expenditure requirements of the government.

5. Finance Bill:

The Finance Bill is introduced in the Parliament along with the Budget, and it provides for the government's tax proposals for the upcoming fiscal year. It includes provisions for new taxes, changes in tax rates, and amendments to the existing tax laws.

6. Expenditure Budget:

The Expenditure Budget is a detailed statement of the government's planned expenditure for the upcoming fiscal year, organized by ministry or department.

7. Receipts Budget:

The Receipts Budget is a statement of the government's expected receipts for the upcoming fiscal year, organized by source, such as tax revenues, non-tax revenues, and borrowings.

Overall, these components of the Union Budget provide a comprehensive overview of the government's economic policies and priorities, as well as its revenue and expenditure plans for the upcoming fiscal year.

J. Union Budget Importance

The Union Budget is an important document for the Indian government and plays a critical role in the country's economic and social development. Here are some reasons why the Union Budget is important:

1. Economic Policy:

The Union Budget is an important tool for the government to outline its economic policies and priorities. It allows the government to allocate resources to various sectors and provide incentives to businesses to stimulate economic growth and development.

2. Resource Allocation:

The Union Budget is the primary tool for the allocation of resources by the government. It allows the government to direct funds towards critical sectors such as health, education, and infrastructure, and to prioritize spending based on the needs of the country

3. Fiscal Discipline:

The Union Budget is also important for maintaining fiscal discipline and macroeconomic stability. The budget outlines the government's revenue and expenditure plans and ensures that the government does not overspend or overborrow, which could lead to inflation and other economic problems.

4. Investor Confidence:

The Union Budget is an important factor in attracting domestic and foreign investment. The budget provides a clear picture of the government's economic policies and priorities, which can help investors make informed decisions about investing in the country.

5. Social Development:

The Union Budget is also important for promoting social development and welfare. The budget allocates funds for various social programs such as health, education, and social security, which can help to reduce poverty and improve the standard of living of the people.

Overall, the Union Budget is a critical tool for the Indian government to promote economic growth and development, maintain fiscal discipline and macroeconomic stability, and promote social development and welfare.

K. STATE BUDGET

In addition to the Union Budget, the individual states in India also prepare their own budgets. The State Budget is a financial plan that outlines the revenue and expenditure for the upcoming fiscal year for a particular state. It is usually presented by the State Finance Minister in the State Legislative Assembly.

The State Budget typically includes the following components:

1. Budget Speech:

The State Finance Minister delivers a speech in the Legislative Assembly outlining the government's economic policies and priorities for the upcoming fiscal year.

2. Annual Financial Statement:

This statement includes details of the government's revenue and expenditure plans for the upcoming fiscal year. It includes the estimates of receipts and expenditure for the year, as well as the manner in which the funds will be raised and spent.

3. Demands for Grants:

The Demands for Grants is a detailed statement of the proposed expenditure of various departments and ministries in the state for the upcoming fiscal year. It includes estimates of the amounts required for each scheme or program, and the justification for the proposed expenditure.

4. Appropriation Bill:

The Appropriation Bill is introduced in the State Legislative Assembly after the State Budget is passed, and it provides for the withdrawal of funds from the Consolidated Fund of the state for meeting the expenditure requirements of the government.

The State Budget is an important tool for the state government to allocate resources and prioritize spending based on the needs of the state. It allows the state government to direct funds towards critical sectors such as health, education, and infrastructure, and to promote social development and welfare. Additionally, the State Budget is important for maintaining fiscal discipline and macroeconomic stability at the state level.

L. IMPORTANCE OF STATE BUDGET

The State Budget is an important document for the state government and plays a critical role in the economic and social development of the state. Here are some reasons why the State Budget is important:

1. Economic Policy:

The State Budget is an important tool for the state government to outline its economic policies and priorities. It allows the government to allocate resources to various sectors and provide incentives to businesses to stimulate economic growth and development.

2. Resource Allocation:

The State Budget is the primary tool for the allocation of resources by the state government. It allows the government to direct funds towards critical sectors such as health, education, and infrastructure, and to prioritize spending based on the needs of the state.

3. Fiscal Discipline:

The State Budget is also important for maintaining fiscal discipline and macroeconomic stability at the state level. The budget outlines the state government's revenue and expenditure plans and ensures that the government does not overspend or overborrow, which could lead to inflation and other economic problems.

4. Social Development:

The State Budget is important for promoting social development and welfare in the state. The budget allocates funds for various social programs such as health, education, and social security, which can help to reduce poverty and improve the standard of living of the people.

5. Investor Confidence:

The State Budget is an important factor in attracting domestic and foreign investment to the state. The budget provides a clear picture of the state government's economic policies and priorities, which can help investors make informed decisions about investing in the state.

Overall, the State Budget is a critical tool for the state government to promote economic growth and development, maintain fiscal discipline and macroeconomic stability, and promote social development and welfare in the state.

M. Finance Commission in India

The Finance Commission is a constitutional body in India that is appointed by the President of India every five years to recommend the distribution of taxes between the Central Government and the State Governments. The Finance Commission plays an important role in ensuring the financial autonomy of the State Governments and in promoting fiscal federalism in the country.

Here are some key facts about the Finance Commission in India:

1. Appointment:

The Finance Commission is appointed by the President of India every five years. The commission is composed of a chairman and four other members.

2. Functions:

The main function of the Finance Commission is to recommend the distribution of taxes between the Central Government and the State Governments. It also recommends grants-in-aid to the State Governments and the criteria for their distribution.

3. Formula:

The Finance Commission uses a formula to determine the share of taxes that should be allocated to each State. The formula takes into account factors such as the State's population, its per capita income, the distance from the national capital, and the level of development.

4. Report:

The Finance Commission submits a report to the President of India, which is laid before both Houses of Parliament. The report contains recommendations on the distribution of taxes, grants-in-aid, and other fiscal matters.

5. Importance:

The Finance Commission plays a crucial role in promoting fiscal federalism in India. It ensures that the State Governments have adequate resources to carry out their functions and promotes the equitable distribution of resources across the country.

Overall, the Finance Commission is an important constitutional body in India that plays a key role in promoting fiscal federalism and ensuring the financial autonomy of the State Governments.

N. Appointment of Finance Commission

The Finance Commission is appointed by the President of India under Article 280 of the Constitution of India. The Finance Commission is appointed every five years, or at such earlier time as the President may specify. The appointment of the Finance Commission is an important process, as the Commission plays a crucial role in determining the distribution of taxes between the Central Government and the State Governments.

Here are the steps involved in the appointment of the Finance Commission:

1. Notification:

The President of India issues a notification specifying the appointment of the Finance Commission.

2. Composition:

The Finance Commission is composed of a Chairman and four other members. The President of India appoints the Chairman and members of the Finance Commission.

3. Terms of Reference:

The President of India also specifies the terms of reference for the Finance Commission. The terms of reference define the scope of the Commission's work and the issues that it is required to address.

4. Duration:

The Finance Commission is appointed for a period of five years, or at such earlier time as the President may specify.

5. Report:

The Finance Commission submits its report to the President of India, which is laid before both Houses of Parliament. The report contains recommendations on the distribution of taxes, grants-in-aid, and other fiscal matters.

Overall, the appointment of the Finance Commission is an important process that is carried out under the provisions of the Constitution of India. The Commission plays a crucial role in promoting fiscal federalism in India and ensuring the financial autonomy of the State

O. FUNCTIONS OF FINANCE COMMISSION IN INDIA

The Finance Commission is a constitutional body in India that is responsible for recommending the distribution of financial resources between the central government and the state governments.

Here are the main functions of the Finance Commission in India:

1. Distribution of Taxes:

The Finance Commission recommends the distribution of taxes between the central government and the state governments. It recommends the percentage of tax revenues that should be allocated to the states and the criteria for their distribution.

2. Grants-in-Aid:

The Finance Commission recommends grants-in-aid to the states to support their developmental needs. These grants can be for specific purposes, such as education or healthcare, or for general purposes.

3. Debt Consolidation:

The Finance Commission recommends measures to consolidate the debts of the states and suggests ways to reduce their interest burden.

4. Fiscal Discipline:

The Finance Commission recommends measures to improve the fiscal discipline of the state governments. It can suggest ways to increase their revenue and reduce their expenditure.

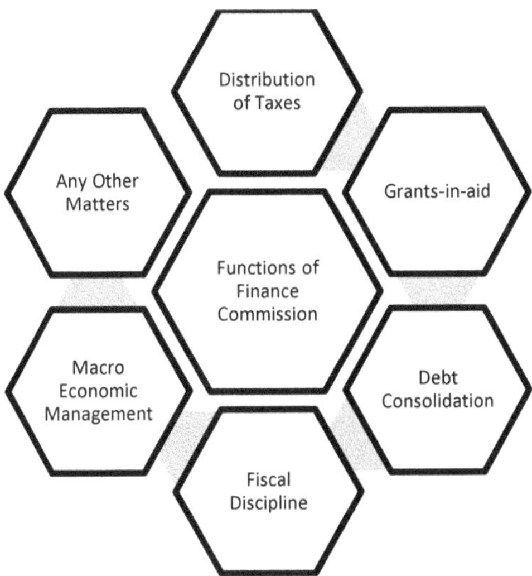

Exhibit5.7: Functions of Finance Commission

5. Macro-Economic Management:

The Finance Commission also recommends measures to improve the macro-economic management of the country. It can suggest ways to control inflation, promote growth, and maintain financial stability.

6. Any other matter:

The Finance Commission is also authorized to make any other recommendations related to the financial relations between the central government and the state governments.

Overall, the Finance Commission plays a critical role in ensuring a fair and equitable distribution of financial resources between the central government and the state governments, and in promoting the development and welfare of the country.

P. MEANING OF STRIKING THE BALANCE BETWEEN INFLATION AND ECONOMIC GROWTH:

Striking the balance between inflation and economic growth refers to the process of managing the economy in such a way that inflation remains under control while economic growth continues to take place.

Inflation is the rate at which the general price level of goods and services in an economy is increasing over time. High inflation can be detrimental to an economy as it reduces the purchasing power of money and leads to a decrease in the standard of living.

On the other hand, economic growth refers to an increase in the production of goods and services in an economy over time. Economic growth can lead to higher levels of employment, increased income, and an improved standard of living.

Thus, striking the balance between inflation and economic growth involves managing the economy in such a way that inflation is kept under control while economic growth continues to take place.

This can be achieved through various policies such as monetary policy, fiscal policy, and supply-side policies. These policies are aimed at promoting economic growth while keeping inflation under control, thereby ensuring a sustainable and stable economy.

Q. CENTRAL GOVT STRIKING BALANCE BETWEEN INFLATION AND ECONOMIC GROWTH WITH THE HELP OF MONETARY POLICIES AND FISCAL POLICIES:

The central government in India employs both monetary and fiscal policies to strike a balance between inflation and economic growth. Here are some ways in which the government is doing this:

1. Monetary Policy:

The Reserve Bank of India (RBI) is responsible for implementing monetary policy in India.

The RBI has been pursuing an accommodative monetary policy stance, which involves keeping interest rates low to stimulate economic growth. This has been done through measures such as keeping the repo rate (the rate at which the RBI lends money to commercial banks) at a low level and providing liquidity to the financial system through various instruments such as open market operations and targeted long-term repo operations.

2. Fiscal Policy:

The central government also employs fiscal policy to manage the economy. The government has increased public expenditure in key areas such as infrastructure development, healthcare, and education to stimulate economic growth. It has also implemented several reforms to improve the ease of doing business in India, which is expected to attract foreign investment and promote economic growth.

3. Supply-Side Measures:

The central government has taken several measures to increase the supply of goods and services in the economy. For instance, it has implemented various schemes to promote entrepreneurship and start-ups, which are expected to create jobs and increase economic activity. It has also implemented measures to increase agricultural productivity, which can increase the supply of food and reduce food prices.

4. Price Controls:

The government has implemented price controls on essential goods such as food and fuel to reduce inflationary pressures. For instance, it has implemented a system of minimum support prices for agricultural produce to ensure that farmers receive a fair price for their produce. It has also capped the prices of certain essential medicines and medical devices to ensure that they are affordable to the general public.

Overall, the central government in India is employing a mix of monetary, fiscal, and supply-side measures to strike a balance between inflation and economic growth. These measures are expected to promote economic growth while ensuring that inflation remains under control.

CHAPTER SUMMARY

FISCAL POLICY

The chapter on Fiscal Policy provides a comprehensive overview of the role of fiscal policy in shaping India's economic framework. It begins by explaining fiscal policy in India, which refers to the government's use of taxation and public spending to influence the economy. The chapter highlights the significance of fiscal policy in promoting economic growth, reducing income inequality, and managing inflation.

The features of fiscal policy in India are explored in detail, showing how the government's budgetary decisions impact different sectors of the economy. The chapter emphasizes the objectives of fiscal policy, including stabilizing the economy, achieving high employment levels, reducing public debt, and fostering sustainable development. These objectives guide the government's decisions on revenue collection and expenditure allocation.

A critical focus of the chapter is on the sources of finance for the state and central governments, which include taxation, borrowing, and non-tax revenues. These financial sources are crucial for funding various public services, infrastructure development, and welfare programs.

The chapter also provides an in-depth explanation of the budget process in India, covering the types of budgets prepared by the Indian government, including Union Budget and State Budget. The importance of Indian government budgets is highlighted, particularly their role in allocating resources to different sectors, ensuring fiscal discipline, and managing public finances.

Additionally, the chapter discusses the Finance Commission in India, its appointment, and its functions in determining how revenues should be distributed between the central and state governments. The Finance Commission plays a pivotal role in ensuring balanced fiscal management across the country.

A key topic in this chapter is the concept of striking the balance between inflation and economic growth. The chapter discusses how the central government, in collaboration with the RBI, uses a combination of fiscal and monetary policies to maintain economic stability, ensuring that inflation is kept in check while promoting growth.

In conclusion, the chapter emphasizes the crucial role of fiscal policy in managing India's economy. It outlines how the government's spending and revenue collection decisions are aimed at balancing economic growth with financial stability, ensuring that public finances are managed responsibly. Through its budgets and fiscal strategies, the government strives to achieve equitable growth and maintain macro-economic stability.

CASE STUDIES

Case Study 5.1: The Role of Fiscal Policy in India's Post-Demonetization Recovery (2016-2017)

In November 2016, India underwent a historic economic event when the government demonetized ₹500 and ₹1,000 currency notes, removing approximately 86% of the cash in circulation. This move aimed to curb black money, counterfeit currency, and corruption, but it also caused significant short-term economic disruptions, particularly for cash-dependent sectors such as small businesses, agriculture, and retail. To mitigate the adverse effects and aid economic recovery, the Indian government, in coordination with the Reserve Bank of India (RBI), introduced a series of fiscal policy measures in the 2016-2017 fiscal year.

One of the primary fiscal responses was an increase in public spending, particularly in infrastructure and rural development projects. The government allocated additional resources to rural employment schemes like the Mahatma Gandhi National Rural Employment Guarantee Act (MGNREGA), which helped provide livelihood support to those in rural areas affected by the cash crunch. By stimulating rural demand through higher public expenditure, the government aimed to offset the economic slowdown caused by demonetization.

In addition to public spending, the government announced tax reforms to encourage greater transparency and formalization of the economy. This included the Pradhan Mantri Garib Kalyan Yojana (PMGKY), a scheme that allowed individuals to deposit unaccounted wealth in bank accounts while paying taxes and penalties, thus integrating more resources into the formal economy. The Goods and Services Tax (GST), implemented in 2017, was another significant fiscal reform that followed demonetization. By creating a unified tax system, GST aimed to simplify tax compliance and reduce the informal sector's dominance in the economy.

The Union Budget 2017-18 also reflected the government's fiscal strategy to support recovery. It included substantial allocations for affordable housing, increased investment in roads and railways, and a focus on digital payments. To address the cash shortage, the government encouraged the adoption of digital financial services, promoting mobile wallets, UPI, and card-based transactions. This push for digitalization was further supported by fiscal incentives for businesses and individuals using digital modes of payment.

The government's fiscal policy response played a crucial role in stabilizing the Indian economy after the initial shock of demonetization. By increasing public spending, introducing tax reforms, and promoting digital financial inclusion, the fiscal measures helped cushion the impact on the most affected sectors and set the stage for economic recovery.

Questions Based on the Case:

i. How did the government's increased public spending, especially in rural development projects, help mitigate the effects of demonetization?

ii. What role did tax reforms like the Pradhan Mantri Garib Kalyan Yojana (PMGKY) play in the formalization of the Indian economy post-demonetization?

iii. How did the government's push for digital financial services contribute to economic recovery following the demonetization event?

Case Study 5.2: Fiscal Policy and the Implementation of the Goods and Services Tax (GST) in 2017

The introduction of the Goods and Services Tax (GST) on July 1, 2017, marked a major fiscal reform in India's taxation system. The GST aimed to replace multiple cascading taxes levied by the central and state governments, such as excise duty, VAT, service tax, and others, with a single unified tax. This reform was designed to create a common national market, reduce tax evasion, and simplify the indirect tax structure, thereby boosting economic efficiency and compliance.

The Indian government had long recognized the need for a unified tax system to address the complexities of the earlier multi-layered tax structure, which hindered the ease of doing business and led to tax leakages. The GST was intended to create a destination-based tax system, wherein taxes are levied at the point of consumption rather than production, ensuring that the entire supply chain—from manufacturing to retail—fell under one tax regime.

From a fiscal policy perspective, GST was critical in expanding the tax base. One of the primary objectives of introducing GST was to increase government revenue by bringing more businesses and individuals into the tax net. Prior to GST, a significant portion of the economy operated in the informal sector, avoiding taxes. GST aimed to promote formalization by encouraging small businesses to register under the tax system, thus reducing the informal economy and boosting tax compliance.

The Union Government, in coordination with the GST Council, a body comprising central and state finance ministers, played a crucial role in designing and implementing the GST framework. The introduction of a four-tier tax structure with rates of 5%, 12%, 18%, and 28% helped categorize goods and services based on their necessity or luxury status. Essential items such as food were either exempt from GST or taxed at a lower rate, while luxury goods and sin products attracted higher rates.

While GST promised long-term benefits, its immediate implementation faced significant challenges. Businesses initially struggled with compliance due to the complex filing system and the need for digital infrastructure. Small and medium-sized enterprises (SMEs), in particular, found it difficult to adapt to the new system. To address these concerns, the government introduced simplified tax returns and extended deadlines to ease the transition process for businesses.

Despite the initial hurdles, the GST reform proved to be a pivotal step toward creating a more streamlined and efficient tax system in India. The introduction of input tax credit, which allowed businesses to claim credits for the taxes paid on inputs, helped reduce the overall tax burden, making Indian businesses more competitive in the global market.

Questions Based on the Case:

i. How did the introduction of GST simplify the indirect tax system in India and promote the creation of a common national market?

ii. What role did the GST Council play in implementing the tax, and how did it address the concerns of different states and industries?

iii. How did GST help in expanding India's tax base and promote the formalization of the economy, especially among small and medium-sized enterprises (SMEs)?

Case Study 5.3: Fiscal Policy and the Indian Government's Response to COVID-19 Pandemic (2020-2021)

The COVID-19 pandemic had a profound impact on India's economy, resulting in one of the sharpest economic contractions in decades. To address the economic fallout, the Indian government deployed a comprehensive set of fiscal policy measures as part of the Atmanirbhar Bharat (Self-Reliant India) Package. This fiscal stimulus aimed to support businesses, individuals, and sectors severely impacted by the pandemic, while also boosting demand and economic recovery.

At the heart of this fiscal response was an economic package amounting to ₹20 lakh crore, which included a combination of direct government spending, financial guarantees, and regulatory reforms. A significant part of the package focused on providing liquidity to businesses, especially Micro, Small, and Medium Enterprises

(MSMEs), which were among the hardest-hit sectors. The government rolled out credit guarantees to banks to encourage lending to MSMEs, along with subsidized interest rates to ease their financial burdens.

The fiscal package also included direct cash transfers to vulnerable sections of the population through schemes like the Pradhan Mantri Garib Kalyan Yojana (PMGKY). Under this scheme, the government provided free food grains to low-income families and direct cash transfers to women, senior citizens, and farmers. This was aimed at ensuring basic sustenance for those severely affected by the pandemic-induced lockdowns.

Furthermore, the government introduced tax relief measures to provide businesses with financial breathing space. The deadlines for filing taxes were extended, penalties were reduced, and some businesses were granted temporary tax waivers. The government also reduced the TDS (Tax Deducted at Source) rates, which allowed businesses to retain more cash in hand.

The agriculture sector was also a critical focus of the fiscal response. Recognizing its importance as the backbone of the rural economy, the government announced several fiscal measures to improve supply chains, infrastructure, and market access for farmers. Investment in agricultural infrastructure was scaled up, and farmers were offered additional credit support to stabilize their incomes and reduce distress during the pandemic.

The Union Budget 2021-22 further reflected the government's long-term fiscal strategy to promote economic recovery. The budget increased capital expenditure on health, infrastructure, and rural development, with a particular focus on enhancing healthcare infrastructure in response to the pandemic. Additionally, sectors like manufacturing, construction, and real estate were targeted with specific fiscal incentives to boost investment and employment.

The Indian government's fiscal response to the pandemic, particularly through its Atmanirbhar Bharat package, helped stabilize the economy in the short term, providing relief to businesses and vulnerable populations. Although challenges remained, especially in terms of timely implementation and disbursement, these fiscal measures played a crucial role in mitigating the economic damage caused by the pandemic and setting the stage for recovery.

Questions Based on the Case:

i.   How did the Indian government's fiscal stimulus through the Atmanirbhar Bharat package support MSMEs and promote liquidity during the COVID-19 pandemic?

ii.   What role did direct cash transfers and food distribution programs play in alleviating the distress of low-income families during the pandemic?

iii. How did the fiscal measures introduced by the government in response to COVID-19 help stabilize the agriculture sector and rural economy?

Case Study 5.4: Fiscal Policy and the Introduction of the Pradhan Mantri Jan Dhan Yojana (PMJDY)

Launched in 2014, the Pradhan Mantri Jan Dhan Yojana (PMJDY) was a significant fiscal policy initiative by the Government of India aimed at enhancing financial inclusion in the country. The objective of this scheme was to provide every Indian household, especially those from low-income and rural backgrounds, access to basic financial services, such as savings accounts, insurance, credit, and pension facilities. The initiative was part of the broader agenda to integrate the unbanked population into the formal financial system, which would enable better government subsidy disbursement, reduce poverty, and promote economic equity.

One of the key aspects of the PMJDY was the opening of zero-balance bank accounts, which allowed individuals who traditionally lacked access to banking services to create accounts without the need for a minimum balance. These accounts were linked to Aadhaar cards, ensuring seamless identity verification and enabling direct benefit transfers (DBTs) from the government. This measure ensured that subsidies, such as LPG gas subsidies or welfare pensions, could be credited directly into the bank accounts of beneficiaries, thereby reducing corruption and leakage in government welfare programs.

The scheme also provided beneficiaries with a RuPay debit card, which could be used for transactions and withdrawals. Moreover, account holders were offered an accidental insurance cover of ₹1 lakh and, in some cases, a life insurance cover of ₹30,000, further enhancing the social security net for low-income individuals.

The fiscal policy impact of PMJDY was multifaceted. Firstly, by bringing millions of previously unbanked individuals into the formal financial system, the government was able to reduce the informal economy and increase tax compliance. Secondly, the scheme helped promote savings habits among the poor, allowing them to participate more actively in the economy. Thirdly, the direct transfer of government benefits into bank accounts helped reduce corruption, as it eliminated intermediaries and ensured that beneficiaries received the full amount of their entitlements.

By 2020, over 400 million accounts had been opened under the PMJDY, reflecting the massive scale and success of the program. However, challenges such as account dormancy and limited financial literacy among beneficiaries persisted. Many account holders did not actively use their accounts for transactions, and the lack of awareness about financial products like insurance and credit limited the scheme's overall impact.

Nevertheless, PMJDY became a cornerstone of India's financial inclusion efforts, laying the foundation for other government schemes like Jan Suraksha, which offered insurance and pension services, and Pradhan Mantri MUDRA Yojana, which provided credit to micro-entrepreneurs. In times of crises, such as the COVID-19 pandemic, PMJDY accounts became crucial for delivering emergency relief funds directly to vulnerable sections of the population.

Questions Based on the Case:

i.   How did the Pradhan Mantri Jan Dhan Yojana contribute to enhancing financial inclusion in India, particularly for low-income households?

ii.   In what ways did the PMJDY support government efforts to reduce corruption and improve the efficiency of welfare distribution?

iii.   What were some of the key challenges faced by the government in ensuring the long-term usage and sustainability of Jan Dhan accounts?

Case Study 5.5: Fiscal Policy and Goods and Services Tax (GST) Implementation in India

The implementation of the Goods and Services Tax (GST) in 2017 was one of the most significant fiscal policy reforms in India's recent history. GST aimed to create a unified national tax by replacing a complex web of multiple indirect taxes, including Value Added Tax (VAT), excise duty, service tax, and others, levied by both the central and state governments. The new tax regime was designed to simplify the indirect tax system, boost compliance, reduce tax evasion, and increase government revenues.

GST was introduced with the promise of "One Nation, One Tax", which was intended to transform India into a single market by eliminating the cascading effect of taxes (tax on tax) that plagued the previous system. It was a destination-based tax and applied at every stage of production and distribution, based on the value-added principle. This change brought uniformity and transparency to the taxation process, reducing the tax burden on end consumers.

The reform introduced a four-tier tax structure with rates of 5%, 12%, 18%, and 28%, depending on the nature of goods and services. Essential items like food were placed under the lower tax brackets, while luxury goods and demerit items such as tobacco and alcohol were taxed at higher rates. Additionally, GST Council, a unique body representing both the central and state governments, was established to make decisions on tax rates, exemptions, and regulations. This collaborative decision-making mechanism was crucial in maintaining fiscal federalism, balancing both central and state interests.

From an economic standpoint, the introduction of GST had several implications. For businesses, GST simplified compliance procedures through the introduction of the Goods and Services Tax Network (GSTN), an online platform for filing tax returns, payments, and refunds. It reduced logistical inefficiencies and cut down on the time taken for the movement of goods across state borders by removing internal tariffs. The tax reform also created an input tax credit mechanism, which allowed businesses to claim credits for the taxes paid on inputs, effectively reducing the overall tax burden and encouraging more formalized business practices.

However, the transition to GST was not without its challenges. Initially, many businesses faced technical difficulties with the GSTN portal and struggled with the complexities of filing monthly and annual returns. Small and medium enterprises (SMEs), in particular, found it difficult to adapt to the new tax system due to limited resources and lack of clarity on certain provisions. Furthermore, several sectors, such as real estate and textiles, experienced disruptions in their supply chains and cash flow issues in the immediate aftermath of GST implementation.

Despite these challenges, GST has led to long-term fiscal benefits for the Indian economy. It increased tax collections by widening the tax base and reducing tax evasion through enhanced transparency and compliance. Over time, GST has contributed to ease of doing business in India, fostering a more integrated and formal economy. Additionally, it has helped to strengthen fiscal federalism by creating a common tax framework that involves both the central and state governments.

Questions Based on the Case:

i. How did the introduction of GST simplify the indirect tax system in India, and what were the key benefits for businesses and consumers?

ii. What were some of the major challenges faced by small and medium enterprises (SMEs) during the transition to the GST regime?

iii. In what ways did the establishment of the GST Council contribute to maintaining fiscal federalism in India?

Key Words

Central bank:

A financial institution responsible for managing a country's monetary policy, regulating commercial banks, and controlling the nation's money supply.

Reserve Bank of India:

The central bank of India responsible for maintaining price stability and ensuring adequate credit flow in the economy.

Monetary policy:

The process by which a central bank controls the supply of money in an economy to achieve its macroeconomic objectives.

Open market operations:

The purchase or sale of government securities by a central bank to influence the money supply and interest rates in the economy.

Money supply:

The total amount of money in circulation in an economy, including cash and bank deposits.

Inflation:

The rate at which the general level of prices for goods and services is rising and, consequently, purchasing power is falling.

Interest rates:

The cost of borrowing or the return on lending money, expressed as a percentage of the amount borrowed or lent.

Bank reserves:

The amount of money that commercial banks hold in reserve to meet depositor withdrawals and to satisfy reserve requirements set by the central bank.

Credit policy:

The set of measures and instruments used by a central bank to regulate the availability and cost of credit in the economy.

Fiscal policy:

The use of government spending, taxation, and borrowing to influence the economy.

Budgets:

A financial plan that outlines expected income and expenses for a given period, typically one year.

Union budget:

The annual financial statement presented by the Government of India in Parliament, outlining its revenue and expenditure for the upcoming fiscal year.

State budget:

The annual financial statement presented by the state governments in their respective legislative assemblies, outlining their revenue and expenditure for the upcoming fiscal year.

Finance Commission:

A constitutional body set up by the Government of India to recommend the distribution of tax revenues between the central government and the state governments.

Macroeconomics:

The branch of economics that studies the performance and behavior of an economy as a whole, rather than individual markets or sectors.

Microeconomics:

The branch of economics that studies the behavior of individuals and firms in making decisions about the allocation of scarce resources.

Gross Domestic Product (GDP):

The total value of goods and services produced within a country's borders in a given period.

Inflation rate:

The percentage increase in the general level of prices of goods and services over a given period.

Consumer Price Index (CPI):

A measure of the average change in the prices of a basket of goods and services consumed by households over a given period.

Repo rate:

The rate at which a central bank lends money to commercial banks in exchange for government securities.

Reverse repo rate:

The rate at which commercial banks can park excess funds with the central bank in exchange for government securities.

Cash reserve ratio (CRR):

The percentage of deposits that commercial banks are required to hold with the central bank as reserves.

Statutory liquidity ratio (SLR):

The percentage of deposits that commercial banks are required to hold in the form of liquid assets, such as government securities.

Non-performing assets (NPAs):

Loans or advances that are in default or have not been serviced by the borrower for a certain period of time.

Base rate:

The minimum rate at which a commercial bank can lend to its customers.

Marginal cost of funds-based lending rate (MCLR):

The minimum interest rate that a bank can charge on loans, determined by its marginal cost of funds.

Capital adequacy ratio (CAR):

The ratio of a bank's capital to its risk-weighted assets, used to determine its ability to absorb losses and maintain solvency.

Monetary Policy:

The process by which a central bank controls the supply of money and credit in an economy to achieve certain macroeconomic objectives such as price stability, full employment, and economic growth.

Open Market Operations:

The purchase or sale of government securities by a central bank to influence the money supply and interest rates.

Repo Rate:

The rate at which a central bank lends money to commercial banks against collateral, usually government securities.

Reverse Repo Rate:

The rate at which a central bank borrows money from commercial banks, usually for short-term periods.

Cash Reserve Ratio:

The percentage of deposits that commercial banks are required to hold with a central bank as reserves.

Statutory Liquidity Ratio:

The percentage of deposits that commercial banks are required to maintain in the form of liquid assets such as government securities.

Bank Rate:

The rate at which a central bank lends money to commercial banks, usually for medium-term periods.

Credit Policy:

The measures taken by a central bank to regulate the availability and cost of credit in an economy.

Capital Adequacy Ratio:

The ratio of a bank's capital to its risk-weighted assets, which is used to measure the bank's ability to absorb losses.

Non-Performing Assets:

Loans and advances that have stopped generating income for a bank due to default or non-repayment.

Asset-Liability Management:

The process of managing a bank's assets and liabilities in a way that minimizes risk and maximizes profit.

Fiscal Policy:

The use of government spending and taxation to influence the economy.

Union Budget:

The annual budget of the central government of India, which outlines its revenue and expenditure plans for the upcoming fiscal year.

State Budget:

The annual budget of a state government in India, which outlines its revenue and expenditure plans for the upcoming fiscal year.

Finance Commission:

A body set up by the Indian government to recommend the distribution of tax revenue between the central and state governments.

Inflation:

The rate at which the general level of prices for goods and services is rising, and subsequently, purchasing power is falling.

Deflation:

The opposite of inflation, where the general level of prices for goods and services is falling, and subsequently, purchasing power is increasing.

Gross Domestic Product (GDP):

The total value of goods and services produced in a country over a specified period, usually a year.

Balance of Payments:

A record of all economic transactions between a country and the rest of the world, including trade, investment, and transfers of money.

Current Account:

The part of a country's balance of payments that records its trade in goods and services, income from abroad, and current transfers

9 798889 556749